the quilt block

~ BIBLE ~

   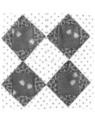  

200+ *traditionally inspired quilt blocks*
from ROSEMARY YOUNGS

KP CRAFT
Cincinnati, Ohio

Contents

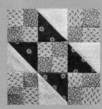

DEDICATION

It is with a heart full of love that I dedicate this book to my loving family.
I love you more than words can ever express. You bless my life every day.

ACKNOWLEDGMENTS

Thank you so much to my dear family—my husband Tom, my children Stacey and her husband Micah, John and his wife Sarah, Amy and her husband Matt, and Jeff, as well as my grandchildren Hailey, Sophia, Dylan, Cecilia, Henry, Josiah, Isaiah and Lydia—for all their love and support.

Thank you to special friends, especially my woman's Bible study at Trinity Reformed Church. Thank you for your friendships, your encouragement, your prayers and for believing in me.

Thank you to all my wonderful quilting and non-quilting friends who are such a special part of my life. We are stitched together by our friendship. Thank you to the donut girls, the Dear Jane group, my wonderful penpals and the Internet quilting groups.

To all the quilters who have inspired me along my journey—whether I have met you at a quilt shop, a retreat, at Beaver Island, Paducah or Shipshewana—thank you so much for your inspiration and friendship.

Thank you to Jennifer Delaney for her beautiful machine quilting expertise.

Thank you to my quilting family and friends who helped me make quilts for this book: Amy Stevens, Sarah Youngs, Hailey Clack, Sophia Clack, Connie Makl, Jeanne Meddaugh, Karen Weilder, Carolyn Vidal, Solomyn Collen and Susan Laity Price.

Thank you to my daughter, Stacey Clack, for her willingness to take the beautiful photographs used in this book.

Thank you to Electric Quilt Company for their willingness to help me with my projects and CDs.

Thank you also to KP Crafts for their confidence and encouragement during the writing of this book, especially to my editors Vanessa Lyman and Kelly Biscopink.

Most importantly, I would like to thank God for the wonderful opportunities and the people I have met through writing, and for always taking the pieces of my life, stitching them together and making something beautiful.

How to Use This Book and CD

When you look at a quilt, what do you see? Do you first see the color, the fabrics, the block patterns or the quilting? Sometimes when we look at quilts, we see different blocks made up of triangles, squares, circles, diamonds and rectangles. Sometimes shapes come together to form stars, baskets, flowers, crosses or pinwheels. The possibilities seem absolutely endless.

The Quilt Block Bible contains 202 historic quilt blocks divided into eight chapters. Each chapter features a different type of block: stars, pinwheels, curves and beyond. Create a quilt using one kind of block (for instance, using all stars), or create a sampler using a variety of block types. Included at the end of the book are instructions for using the blocks to make eleven quilted projects. You'll also find historic quilting tidbits sprinkled throughout the pages.

To use the CD, insert the CD into a computer. Open the PDF file of the block you want to make. Print the file on your home printer, making sure the block prints at 100 percent and is not scaled to fit the page. Measure the printed block; it should measure 6" × 6" (15cm × 15cm). Remember to add ¼" (6mm) seam allowance around all sides of the block. Each block measures 6½" (17cm) unfinished and 6" (15cm) finished. Use the printed page to make templates or prepare a foundation for foundation piecing. Read the *Instructions and Assembly* section for more information on piecing the blocks.

Fabrics, Tools and Supplies

FABRICS: Choosing fabrics is one of my favorite aspects of quilt making. Fabrics with small-scale prints will be most effective since the block is only 6" (15cm) in size when finished. Choose various background and lattice fabrics for different overall effects in the finished quilts.

THREAD: I recommend using a 100-percent cotton 50-weight thread to piece the blocks. This thread resists shrinking and is available in a variety of colors. Use the same thread for appliqué, or substitute a silk thread. For hand quilting, I recommend a strong, 100-percent cotton thread.

SCISSORS: I keep two different pairs of scissors on hand: one for fabric and one for paper.

ROTARY CUTTERS, RULERS AND MAT: I keep two rotary cutters on hand: one to cut fabrics and the other to cut through the fabric once it is sewn to the foundation paper.

SEWING MACHINE NEEDLE: When foundation piecing, use a size-14 sewing machine needle to create an easy-to-tear perforated stitching line.

FOUNDATION PAPER: For foundation piecing, choose a lightweight paper that is both easy to tear away and easy to trace foundations onto. Try different papers to find what you like—newsprint, computer paper or even tracing paper. For printing templates from the CD, be sure to choose a paper that can be run through a printer.

Block Instructions and Assembly

PIECED BLOCK AND APPLIQUÉ TEMPLATE INSTRUCTIONS

Templates are patterns that are used to cut the shapes for a quilt block. They can be used for both hand and machine piecing. I use freezer paper to create templates. Freezer paper is easy to see through to trace the template pieces, and is durable enough to be used several times. The more accurate you are in tracing your templates, the better your block will fit together.

1 Using the CD, print out the block you'd like to make on your printer. Make sure the printout measures 6" × 6" (15cm × 15cm).

2 Place freezer paper over the block printout. Trace all the shapes onto the freezer paper adding a ¼" (6mm) seam allowance on all sides. To be more exact, use a pencil with a thin lead for clear lines. It also helps to number the pieces to keep them in order.

3 Set your iron on the "no steam" setting. Iron the freezer paper onto the right side of your fabric.

4 Cut out all shapes on the ¼" (6mm) line and assemble as shown on the pattern.

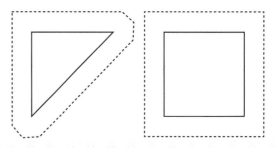

Add ¼" (6mm) seam allowance to all sides of each template shape.

FOUNDATION PIECING INSTRUCTIONS

Foundation piecing is an easy technique for piecing blocks. In this method, fabric is sewn to a paper foundation following a numerical sequence. Sewing lines are copied onto the foundation paper by tracing them with a pencil and adding a $\frac{1}{4}$" seam allowance around each unit. Some of the blocks can be pieced together as a whole unit, as in the examples shown.

1 Decide how many units the pattern will be divided into for piecing.

2 Using a ruler and thin-lead pencil, trace each unit from the printed pattern onto foundation paper. Trace all of the lines of each unit, and add a $\frac{1}{4}$" (6mm) seam allowance around each unit.

3 Number the foundation paper units in the order that the pieces should be sewn together. The more blocks you finish, the easier this will become.

4 Position the first two fabrics right sides together on the unmarked side of the foundation paper.

5 With the marked side of the foundation paper facing up and the fabric on the bottom, stitch on the sewing line between the numbers using a very small stitch; 1.5 will work on most machines.

6 Continue stitching all of the pieces in numerical order until the block or unit is completed. Trim the fabrics so that they are even with the outside line of the foundation. If you have more than one unit for a block, match the units and stitch them together.

7 Keep the foundation papers in place until after the entire quilt top is assembled. Once the top is assembled, gently tear away the foundation papers.

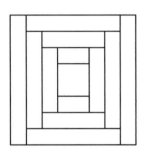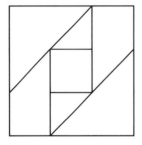

Some blocks can be pieced together as a whole unit.

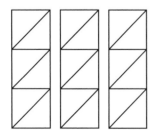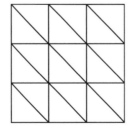

Some blocks need to be pieced together in separate units and then stitched together to make the whole block.

Finishing the Project

All of the projects in this book include specific assembly instructions. Use the following instructions to piece your backing, quilt and bind your project, or to finish your quilt without quilting or binding.

BASTE AND QUILT

1 Remove the selvage from each of the backing sections, cutting $\frac{1}{4}$ " (6cm) past the selvage.

2 Sew the pieces together. Press the seams.

3 Lay the backing right side down on a flat surface, and secure it with tape to keep it flat and taut.

4 Center the batting and quilt top right side up. Thread or pin baste the three layers together.

5 If desired, trim some of the batting and backing, leaving approximately 4" (10cm) around each side of the quilt top.

6 Quilt as desired. Square up the quilt and trim off the excess batting and backing.

BIND THE QUILT

1 Sew the binding strips together at a 45° angle into one long strip. Trim off the excess seam allowance at each seam.

2 With wrong sides together, iron the binding in half along the length of the whole strip.

3 Trim any excess batting and backing fabric even with the edges of the quilt top.

4 Starting in the middle of one side of your quilt, place one end of the binding on top of the quilt, with the raw edges of the binding aligned with the raw edges of the quilt top. Leave the first 3"–4" (8cm–10cm) of the binding strip unstitched, and then stitch the binding to the quilt using ¼" (6mm) seam.

5 As you approach the first corner, stop sewing ¼" (6mm) from the edge of the first corner. With the needle in the down position, turn the quilt and backstitch off the edge.

6 Fold the binding strip away from the corner, making a 45° fold.

7 Holding the fold in place, place the strip back onto the quilt, aligning the raw edge with the next side of the quilt. Pin or hold the fold in place as you continue stitching along the next side of the quilt.

8 Continue stitching the binding to the quilt in this way until you approach the starting point.

9 Stop sewing several inches (5cm–7cm) before you reach your starting point. Overlap both of the loose binding ends where they meet on the quilt.

10 With right sides together, sew the binding ends together at a 45° angle using ¼" (6mm) seam allowance. Trim off the excess seam allowance and binding in the seams and finish stitching the binding to the top of the quilt.

11 Turn the quilt over to the back. Using a blind stitch, sew the binding down on the stitching line by hand, mitering the corners.

MAKE A QUILT BLANKET

1 To finish the quilt without quilting, make a quilt blanket. Pin the backing and quilt top right sides together, making sure there is at least 1" (3cm) of extra backing fabric on all sides of the quilt top.

2 Choose a 6" (15cm) location for an opening where you are going to turn the quilt inside out. Beginning with a backstitch, start sewing on this side. Stitch all the way around your quilt until you arrive at the other end of the opening. Trim the backing even to the size of the quilt top on, except for the area around the opening.

3 Beginning with a backstitch, start sewing on the side where you left the 6" (15cm) opening. Stitch all the way around your quilt until you arrive at the other side of the opening.

4 Turn the quilt right side out through the opening.

5 Tuck under the 6" (15cm) opening and pin. Topstitch around the edge of the entire quilt, being sure to catch the opening's seam allowances in the stitches.

star blocks

S*tar blocks are some of the most popular and versatile blocks used in quilts. There are hundreds of star blocks, many of which have several different interpretations, although sometimes different names have been given to the same star block. Use a simple star block like a Sawtooth or Ohio star, or try a more complicated block like the LeMoyne star in your quilt.*

1. Sawtooth Star
2. Sawtooth Star Variation
3. Shooting Sawtooth Star
4. Star in a Star
5. Stars and Checkerboard
6. Eight-Pointed Star
7. Ohio Star
8. Swamp Angel Star
9. Star X
10. LeMoyne Star
11. LeMoyne Star Variation
12. Aunt Eliza's Star

13. Aunt Eliza's Star Variation
14. Night Moon Star
15. Album Star
16. Album Star Variation
17. Signature Star
18. Mills and Stars
19. Friendship Star
20. Stars and Dot
21. Aunt Nancy's Favorite Star
22. Morning Star
23. Spinning Star
24. Shooting Star

25. Star of Spring
26. Ribbon Star
27. Doris's Delight Star
28. Grandma's Star
29. Radiant Star
30. Old Snowflake Star
31. Star in Square
32. Eccentric Star
33. Sarah's Choice Star
34. Squares and Tulips Star
35. July Fourth Star

Sawtooth Star

A BIT OF HISTORY: Amish quilts are basic in design and are usually pieced together using a treadle sewing machine. Quilts are often made with rich solid colors, black being the most predominant. There are recognizable differences in Amish quilts in their different communities. Other blocks that often appear in Amish quilts are Aunt Eliza's Star (12), Bear Paws (89), Shoofly (108) and Log Cabin (185).

Sawtooth Star Variation

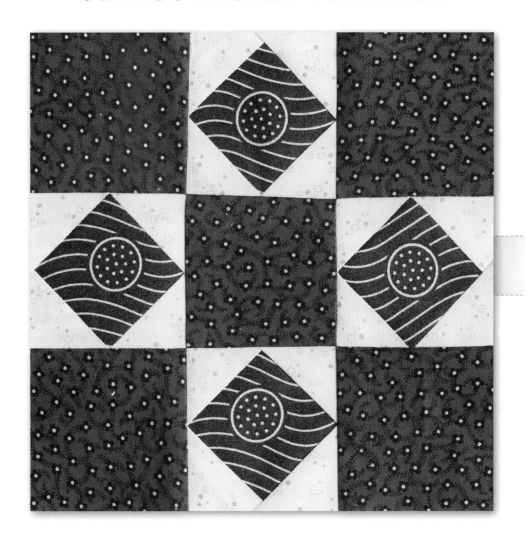

Shooting Sawtooth Star

Star in a Star

Stars and Checkerboard

Eight-Pointed Star

Ohio Star

Swamp Angel Star

Star X

LeMoyne Star

{ **A BIT OF HISTORY** English paper piecing is an old technique that is used to make quilts or quilt blocks by hand. Fabric is basted over a precut paper template, and then the templates are sewn together. This technique is used mostly for sewing hexagons and diamonds and is helpful when constructing the LeMoyne Star.

LeMoyne Star Variation

Aunt Eliza's Star

Aunt Eliza's Star Variation

Night Moon Star

Album Star

Album Star Variation

Signature Star

A BIT OF HISTORY Some signature quilts were used as fundraisers for a particular church or organization. They were even used as fundraisers during wartime to support the troops. The quilt was sold to raise money, and people also had to pay a fee to sign the quilt. In addition to this block, good signature blocks are the Album Star Variation (16) and Double Anchor (158).

Mills and Stars

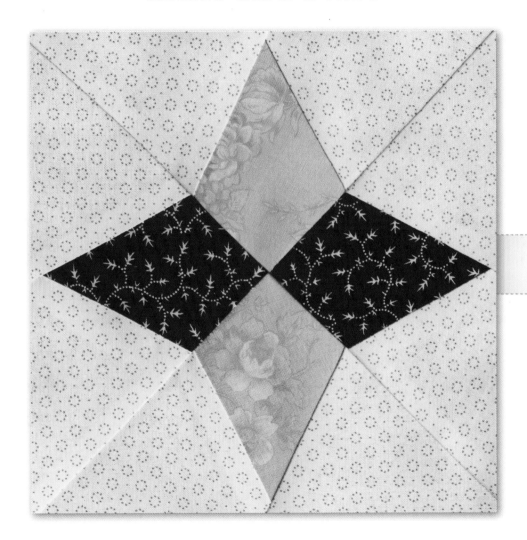

Friendship Star

Stars and Dot

Aunt Nancy's Favorite Star

Morning Star

Spinning Star

Stars

BLOCK
23

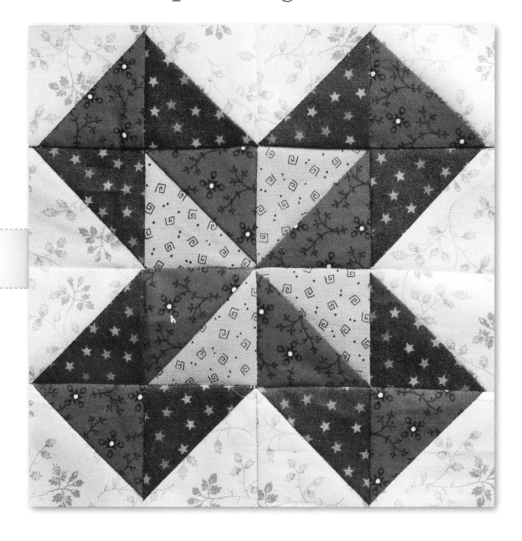

Shooting Star

Star of Spring

Ribbon Star

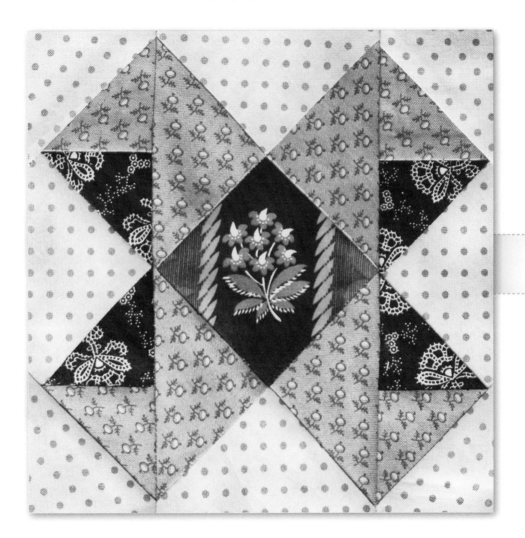

Doris's Delight Star

 DID YOU KNOW? A mourning quilt is made in memory of someone who has died. Sometimes, a mourning quilt is made with the deceased person's clothing. The quilt is intended to comfort the person who experienced the loss. This type of quilt can be made using any quilt block, or a combination of your favorites.

Grandma's Star

Radiant Star

Old Snowflake Star

Star in Square

Eccentric Star

Sarah's Choice Star

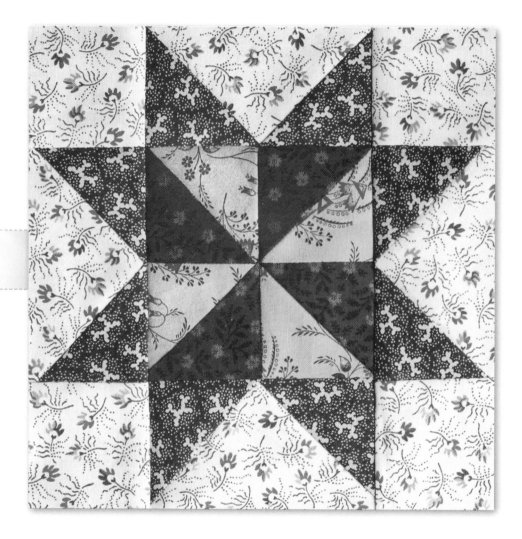

Squares and Tulips Star

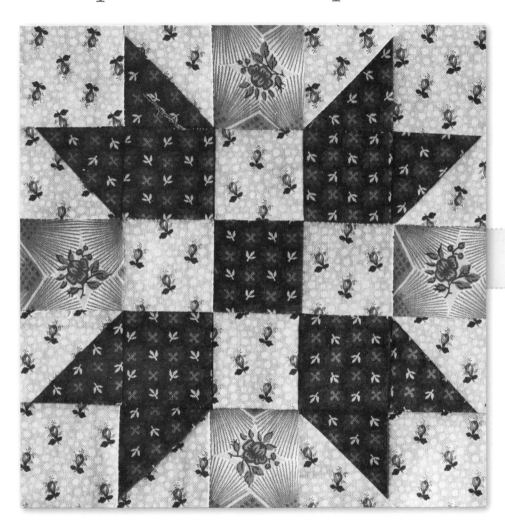

July Fourth Star

{ **A BIT OF HISTORY** The names of quilt blocks can have significant meanings as in July Fourth Star (35) or Red Cross (112). Quilt blocks also have biblical names such as Cross and Crown (118), Jacob's Ladder (123) or Joseph's Coat (144). Some blocks also have political significance, as in Clay's Choice (76) or Mr. Roosevelt's Necktie (80).

2

pinwheels and windmills

Pinwheel and windmill blocks are both traditional quilt blocks, mostly made of triangles that usually show rotation. You can use one of these blocks or a variety of these blocks to create a stunning quilt.

36. Ranger's Pride
37. Whirlpool
38. Pinwheel
39. Whirlwind
40. Fair Pinwheel
41. Dutchman's Puzzle
42. Square Dance
43. Spiderweb
44. Octagons
45. Block Island Puzzle
46. John's Pinwheel

47. Rosebud
48. Wheel of Destiny
49. The Spinner
50. Twirling Pinwheel
51. String Quilt
52. Maltese Cross
53. Key West
54. Crossed Canoes
55. L Windmill
56. Spinning Pinwheel
57. Electric Fan

58. Pinwheel Star
59. Louisiana
60. Scrap Zigzag
61. Twin Sisters
62. Seesaw
63. Geese Squared
64. Four Shooflies
65. Beginner's Delight
66. Windmill
67. Wheels

Ranger's Pride

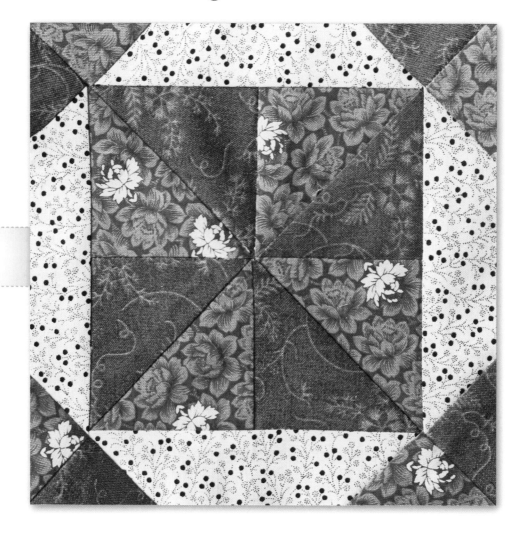

Whirlpool

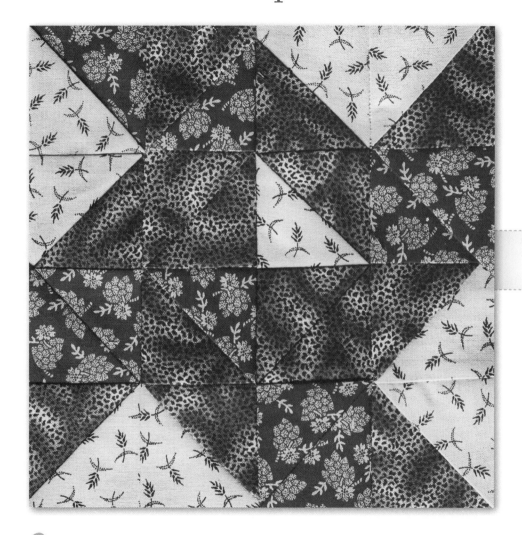

{ **DID YOU KNOW?** Quilts have been pieced using flour or sugar sacks, state fair ribbons and even silk cigar wrappers.

Pinwheel

Pinwheels

BLOCK
38

Whirlwind

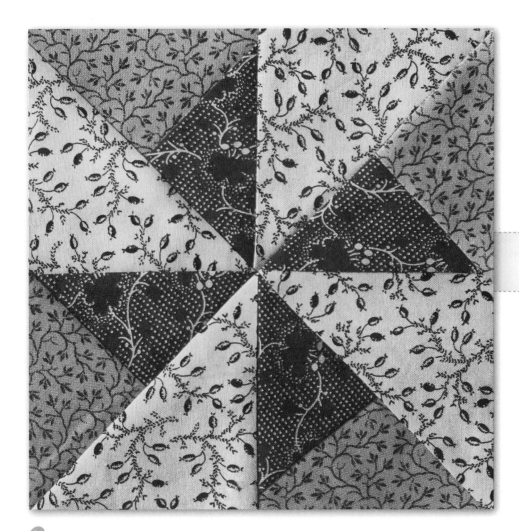

{ **A BIT OF HISTORY** Depression time quilts were usually made with solids and prints in pastel colors. Even though it was such a dark period in the United States, quilts from this period are some of the happiest and most colorful quilts ever made. In addition to this block, other popular block patterns during this time were Friendship Star (19), String Quilt (51), Four Shooflies (64), Simple Nine Patch (98) and Double Patches (101).

Fair Pinwheel

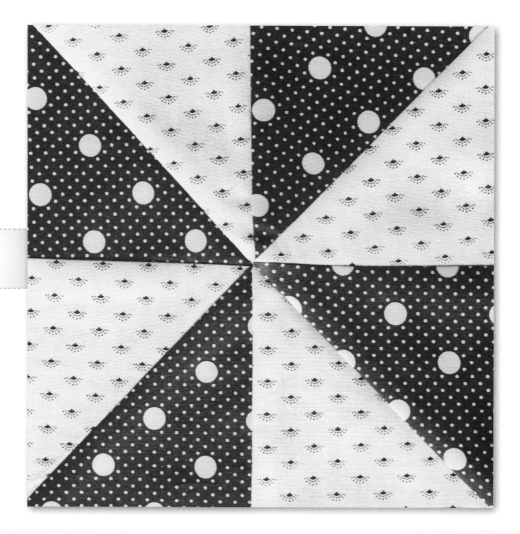

DID YOU KNOW? Redwork embroidery became popular around 1880. Different companies offered penny squares—a muslin square stamped with a redwork embroidery pattern. Penny squares featured pictures of children, animals, flowers or even nursery rhyme figures.

Dutchman's Puzzle

Square Dance

Spiderweb

Octagons

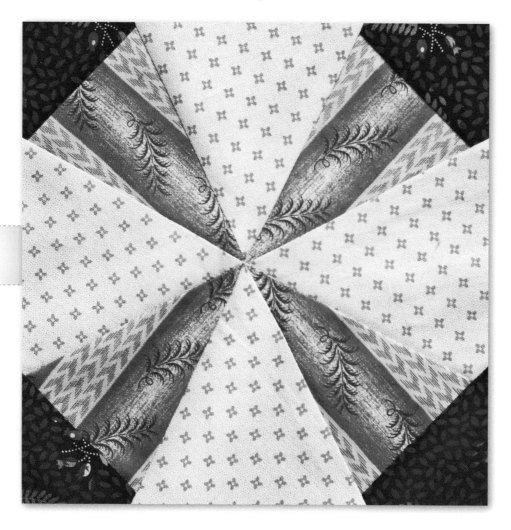

Block Island Puzzle

John's Pinwheel

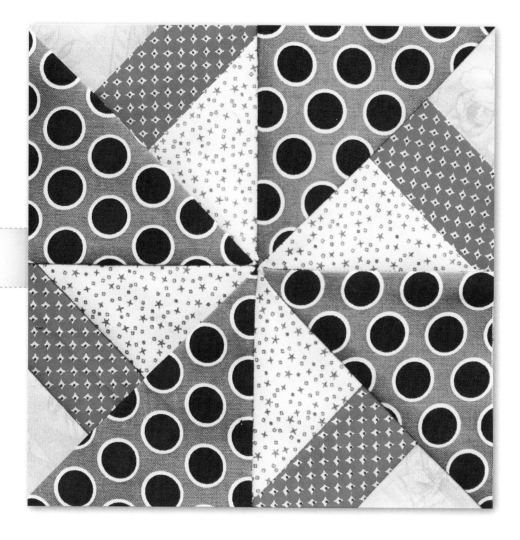

Rosebud

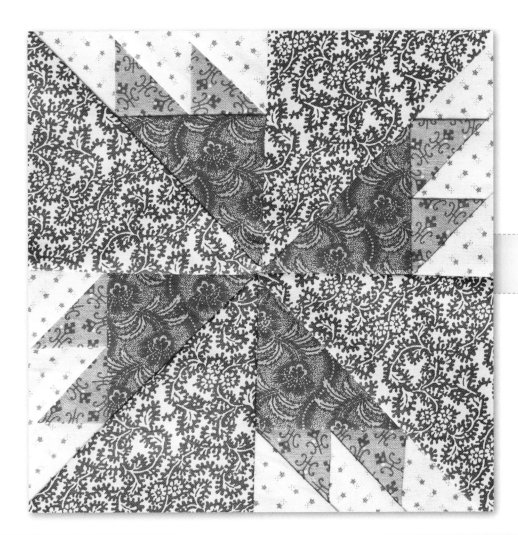

{ **DID YOU KNOW?** Floral appliqué quilts became popular in the 1840s. Most quilters preferred green and red color combinations with large floral motifs. Many of these quilts were made to commemorate a marriage.

59

Wheel of Destiny

The Spinner

Twirling Pinwheel

String Quilt

{ **A BIT OF HISTORY** String quilts were usually made with fabrics from a scrap bag. Strips of fabric were stitched on muslin or old newspapers, and then trimmed to form a segment of the block. Multiple units were then sewn together to form the block.

Maltese Cross

Key West

Crossed Canoes

L Windmill

Spinning Pinwheel

{ **DID YOU KNOW?** Printed patchwork or "cheater cloth" appeared in the 1840s and is still available in quilt shops today. The fabric sometimes was used on the back of quilts and imitated the appearance of a pieced quilt top.

Electric Fan

Pinwheel Star

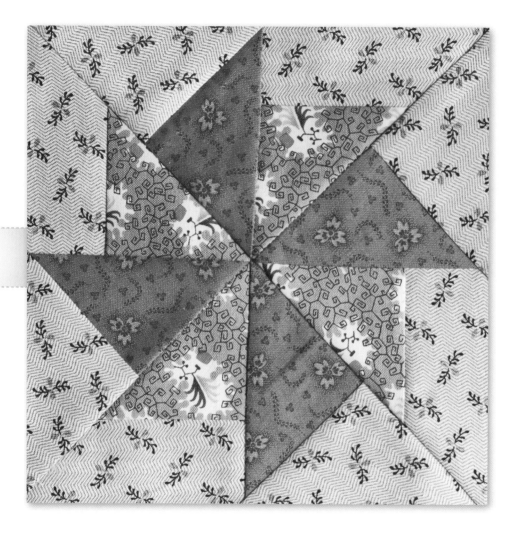

Louisiana

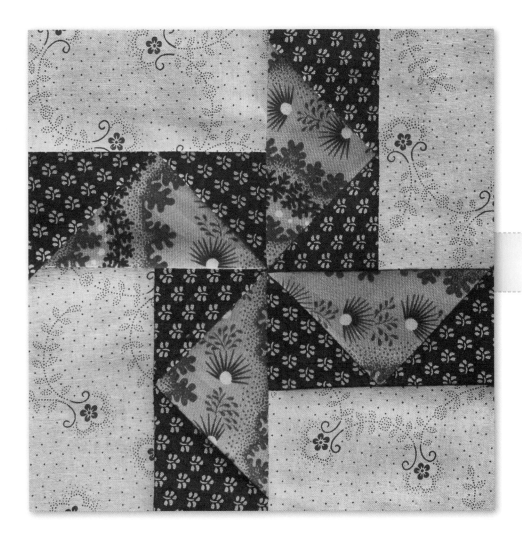

Scrap Zigzag

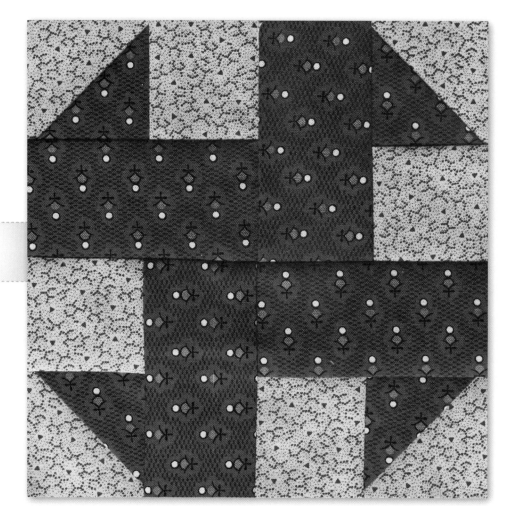

Twin Sisters

Seesaw

Geese Squared

Four Shooflies

{ **A BIT OF HISTORY** Charm quilts became popular in the late 1800s. Women would gather as many pieces of fabric as they could to make their quilt, trying not to repeat any of the fabrics. Blocks that can be used to make charm quilts are Checkerboard (197), Shooting Sawtooth Stars (3), H Block (69), Sixteen Patch (93) and Simple Nine Patch (98).

Beginner's Delight

Windmill

Wheels

four patch blocks

Four patch blocks usually contain four equal sections comprised of squares, rectangles or triangles. Four patch blocks are usually some of the easiest blocks to make: easy to cut and easy to piece together. Try combining two different four patch blocks together in one quilt.

Four Patch

H Block

Zigzag

{ **DID YOU KNOW?** In the 1920s and 1930s, newspapers began to print weekly quilt columns. Sometimes, the columns featured contests using the provided patterns, but most frequently focused on redwork or embroidery. Quilters waited patiently for their newspaper to arrive and then transferred the embroidery pattern onto fabric using carbon paper.

A Square in Squares

Mosaic Geese

Dutchman's Wheel

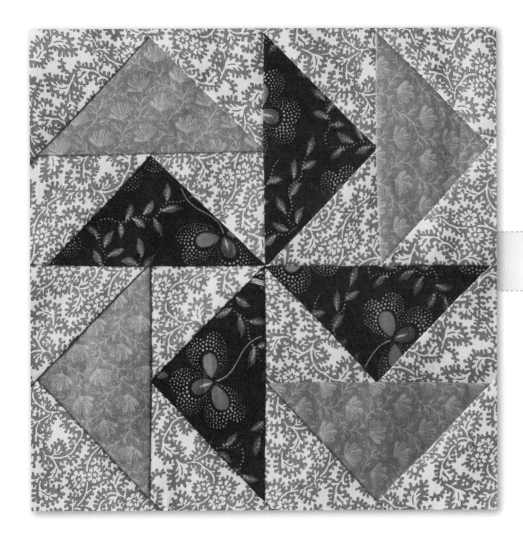

Four Rows of Four Patch

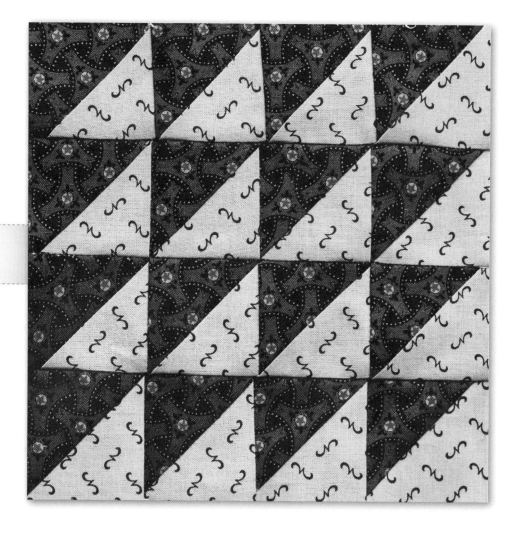

Susannah

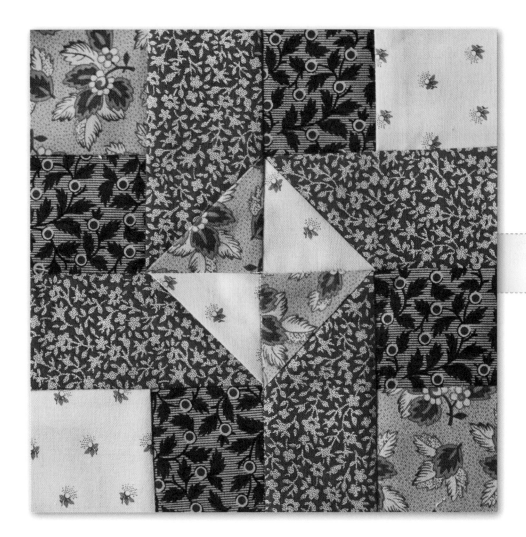

Clay's Choice

{ **A BIT OF HISTORY** Clay's Choice was named after Henry Clay—an American politician in the 1800s. Clay was a congressman and senator and ran twice unsuccessfully for the United States presidency.

Crossroads

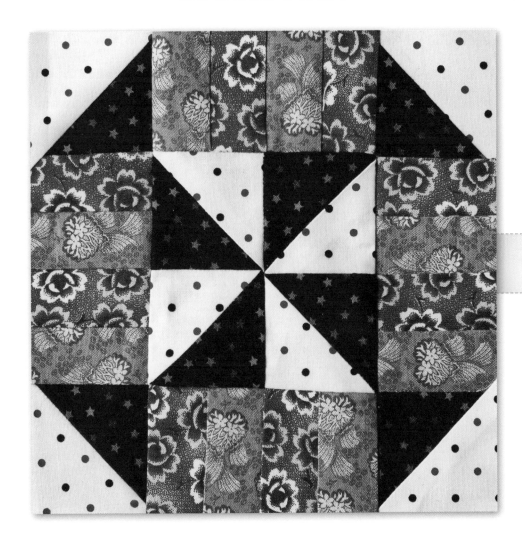

Simple Triangles

4-patches

BLOCK
78

Hourglass

Mr. Roosevelt's Necktie

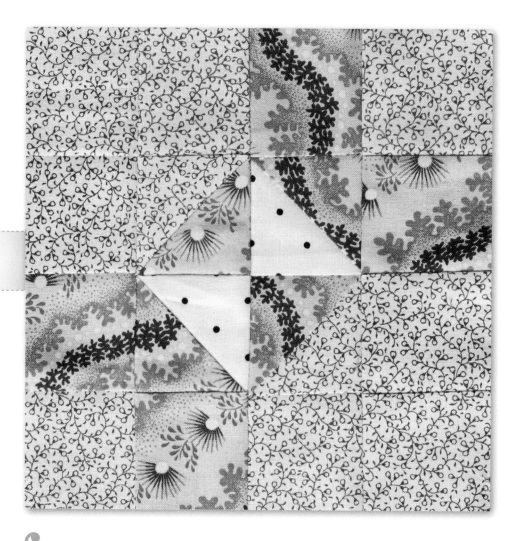

{ **A BIT OF HISTORY** Theodore Roosevelt, or Teddy, as he was known, was the 26th president of the United States. This necktie quilt block represents the necktie that Teddy Roosevelt wore.

Broken Sash

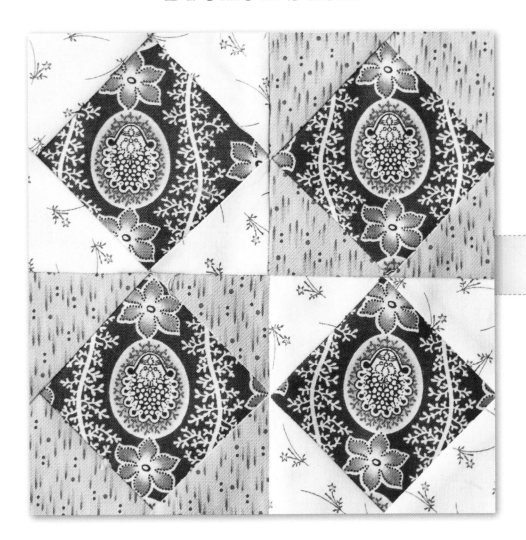

Flock of Geese

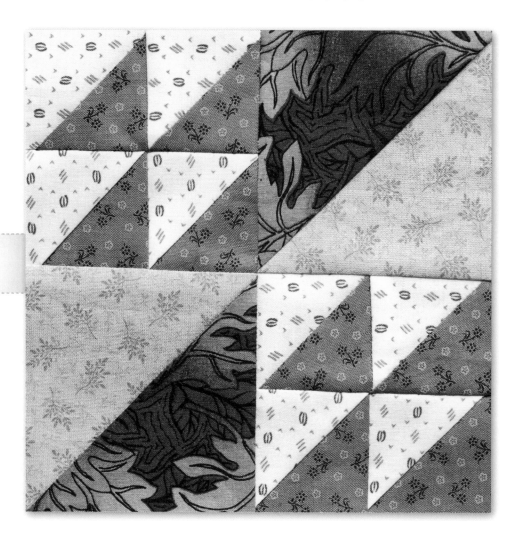

Oklahoma

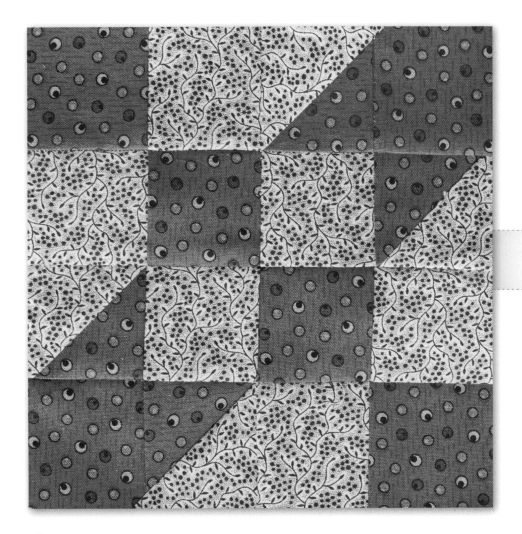

{ **A BIT OF HISTORY** Some quilt blocks are named after notable places, like this block named for Oklahoma. A few other examples are Louisiana (59), Road to California (122), Indiana Puzzle (141), New Jersey (157), Key West (53) and Ohio Star (7).

The Little Cedar Tree

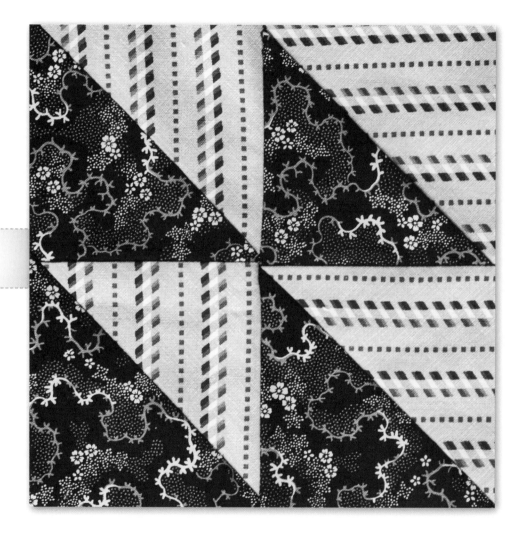

Aircraft

Four Patch Fox and Geese

Goose Creek

This and That

4-patches

BLOCK

88

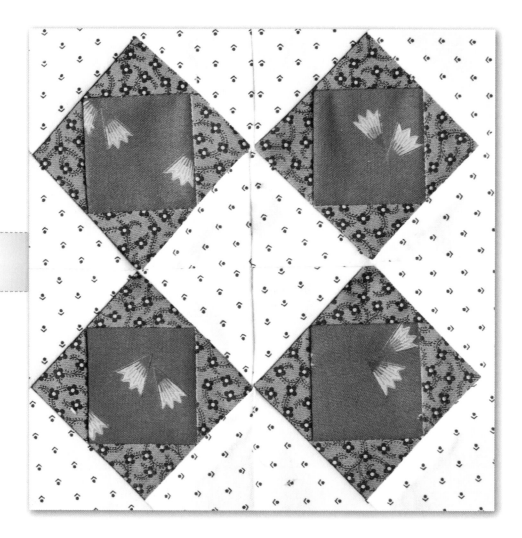

Bear Paws

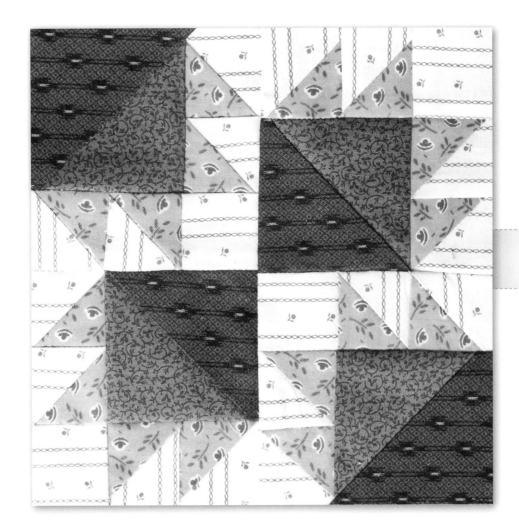

Pinwheels and Squares

Arrows

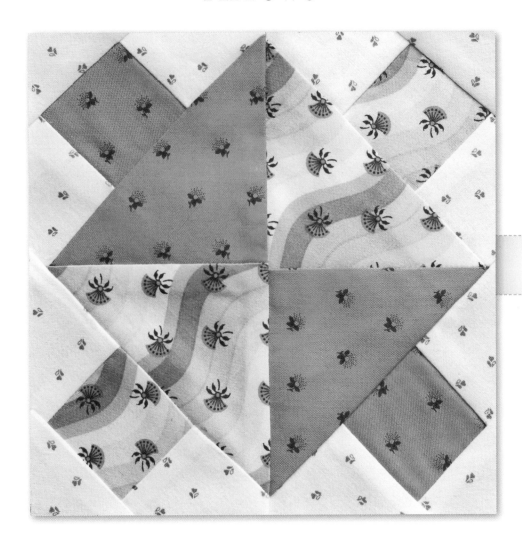

The Anvil

Sixteen Patch

{ **A BIT OF HISTORY** Postage stamp quilts are usually made entirely of small squares about the size of a postage stamp. Sometimes, this block is used to form a design that radiates out from the center, known as a Trip Around the World. Postage stamp quilts are somewhat like a charm or scrap quilt but definitely showcase a quilter's patience.

Four Patch Triangles

4-patches

BLOCK

94

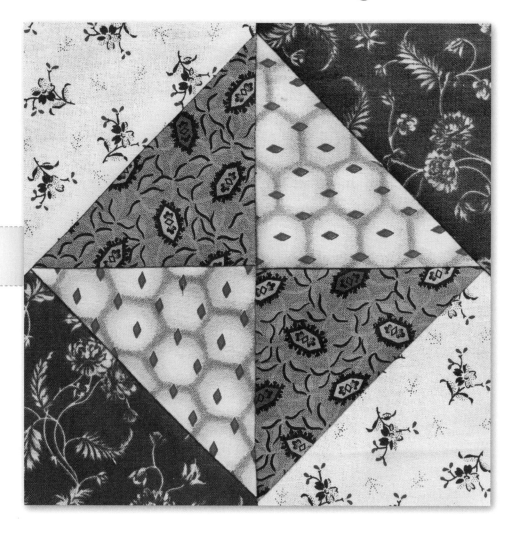

Borrow and Lend

Bowtie

4-patches

BLOCK
96

Rosebuds

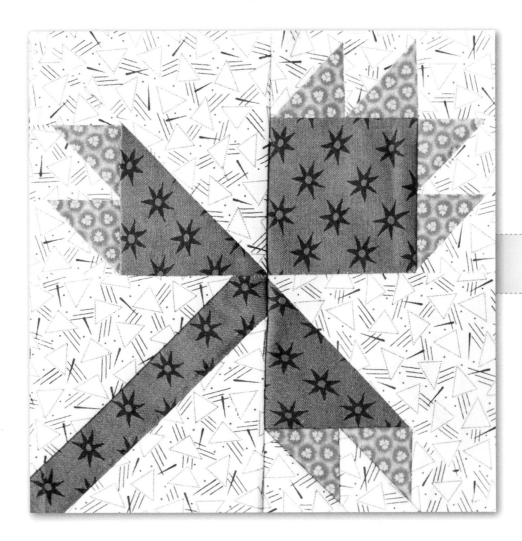

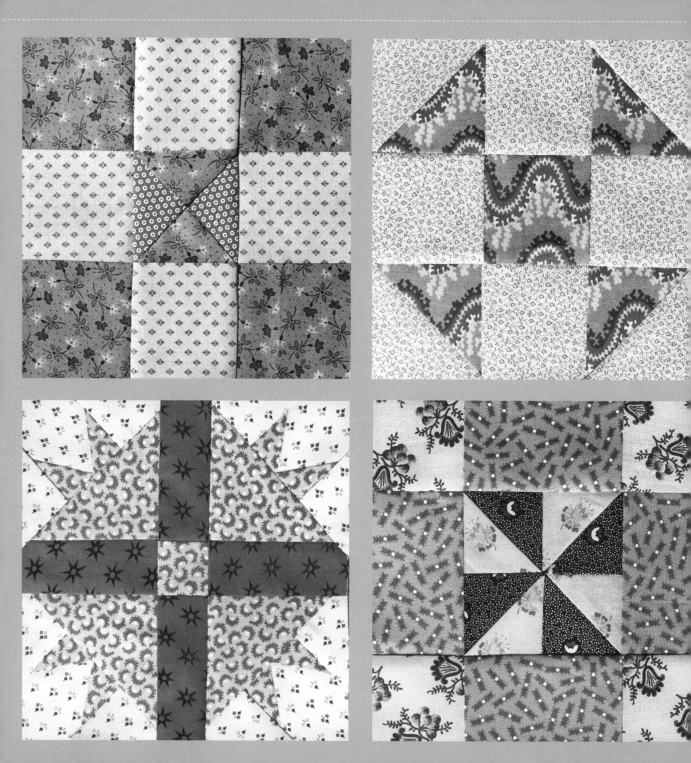

nine patch blocks

One of the earliest forms of patchwork is the nine patch block. It is made by sewing five dark pieces of fabric with four light pieces of fabric, alternating the pieces. It is a great block for a beginner to work with. The nine patch block has many variations, because each of the nine squares that make up the block can be made up of different geometrical shapes.

Simple Nine Patch

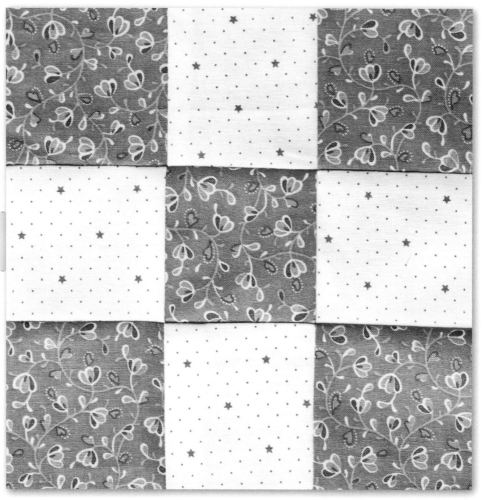

{ **A BIT OF HISTORY** In the 1930s, quilters used colorful feed sacks in their quilts. As a quilter was buying animal feed or flour, she could pick out what feed sacks she wanted. Appliqué blocks such as Sun Bonnet Sue and butterflies appeared in many feed sack quilts. Hexagons, Dresden plates and wedding ring quilts were also popular. Other blocks that were frequently used in feed sack quilts were Spiderweb (43), Pinwheel Star (58) and Log Cabin (185).

Nine Patch

Double Nine Patch

Double Patches

Maple Leaf

Chinese Coins

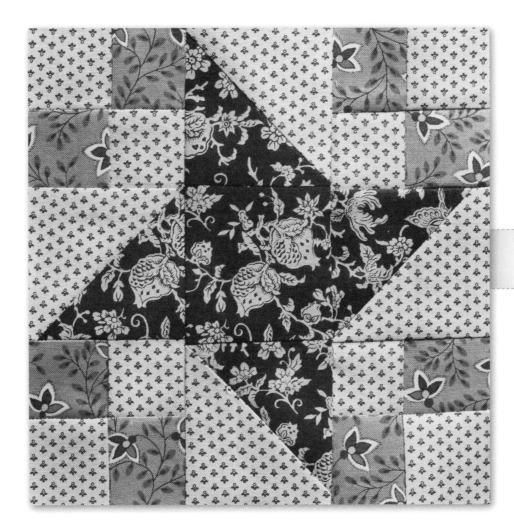

Double X

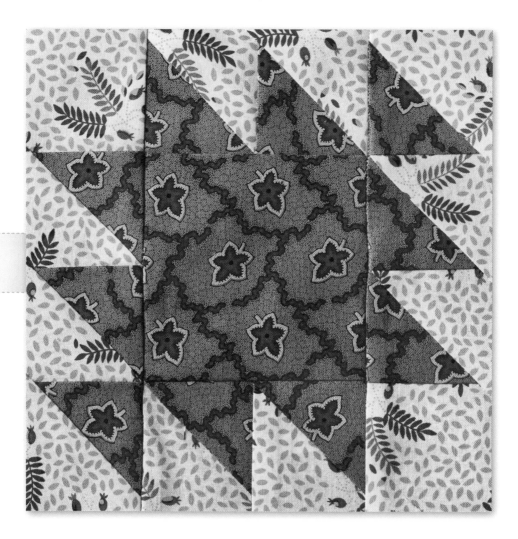

Puss in the Corner

Blockhouse

Square-in-Square Puzzle

Shoofly

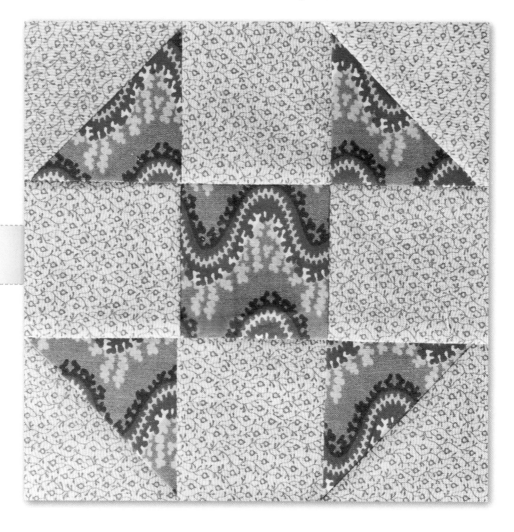

New Album

Rail Fence

Forest Path

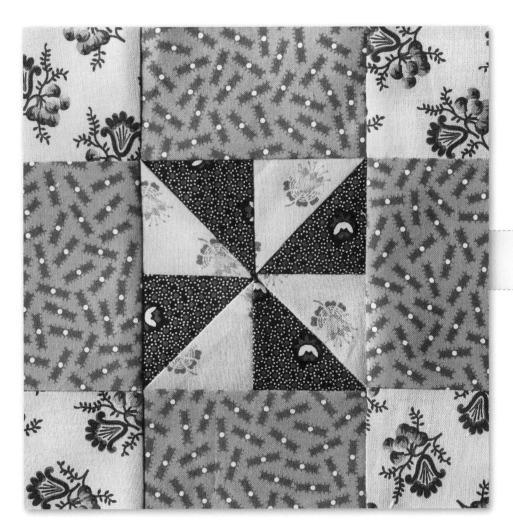

Red Cross

A BIT OF HISTORY The Red Cross was founded by Clara Barton in the late 1800s. The Red Cross provides relief to members of the armed forces and helps reduce the loss of life and property by lessening the impact of national and international disasters.

Dragon Head

Patchwork

9-patches

BLOCK
114

Simple Hourglass

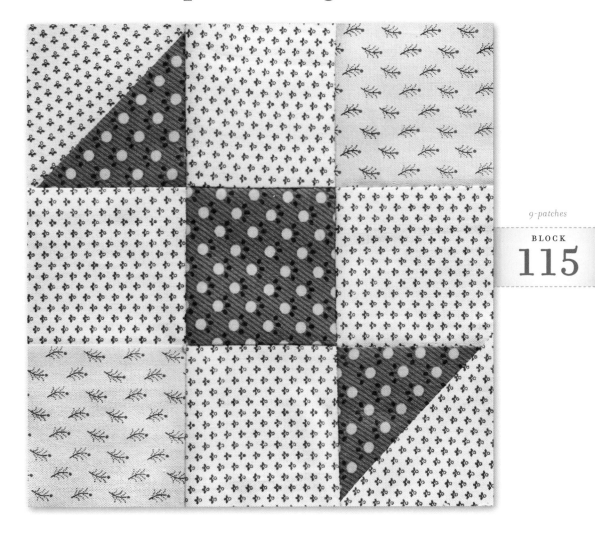

9-patches

BLOCK
115

Nine Patch Windows

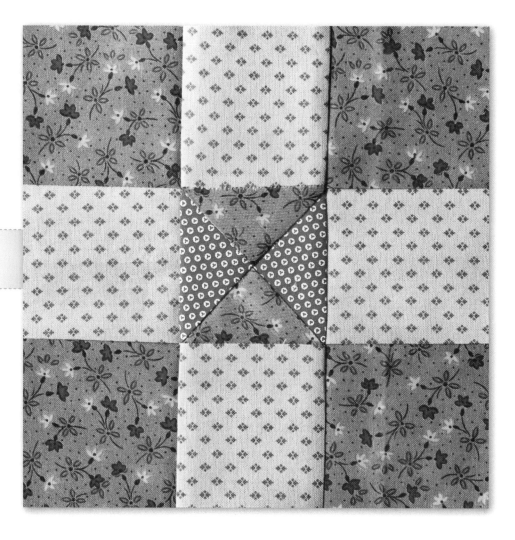

King's Crown

Cross and Crown

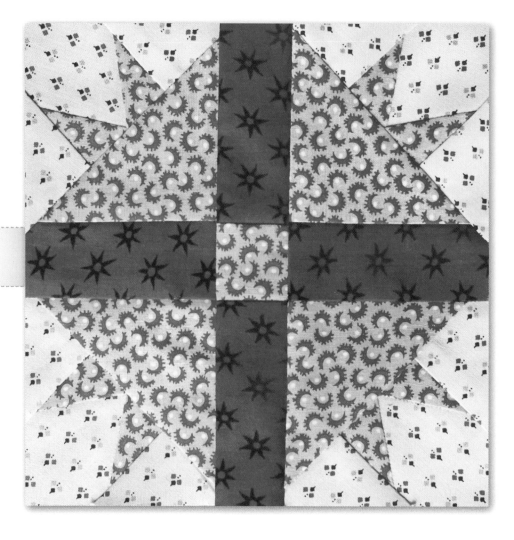

9-patches

BLOCK
118

Wild Geese

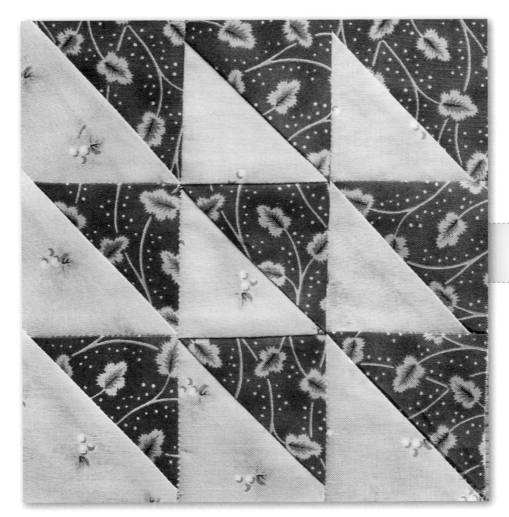

Mosaic

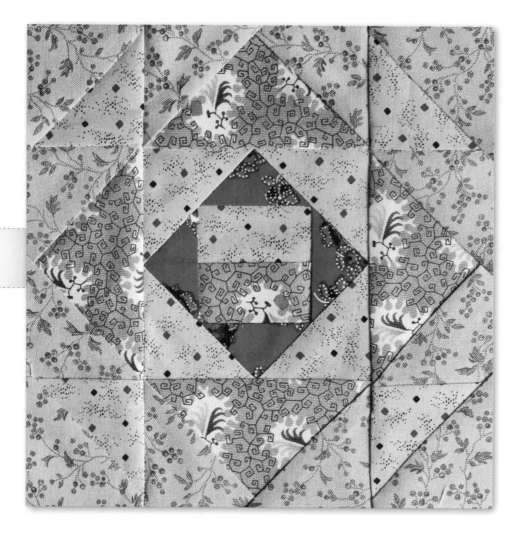

Crowns of Triangles

9-patches

BLOCK

121

Road to California

9-patches

BLOCK
122

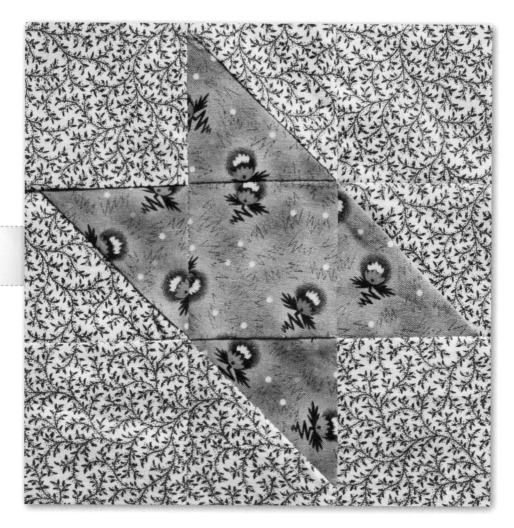

Jacob's Ladder

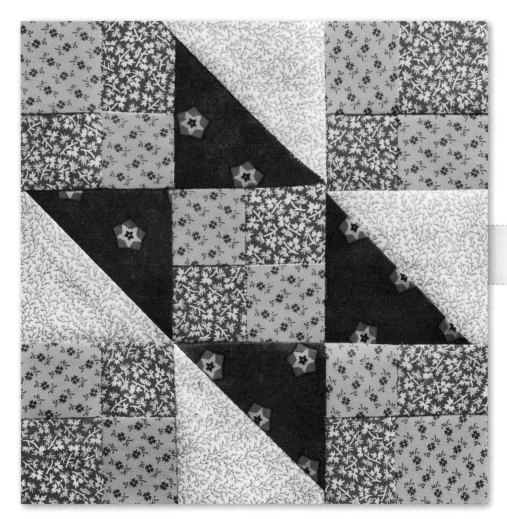

Spool

Hourglass Nine Patch

Big T

9-patches

BLOCK
126

DID YOU KNOW? The United States Sanitary Commission was formed to help the sick and wounded in the United States Army during the Civil War. In addition to medical supplies and food, they distributed thousands of quilts and blankets to the soldiers.

Friendship Square

Maze

Grandmother's Choice

Crazy Ann

Cross in Square

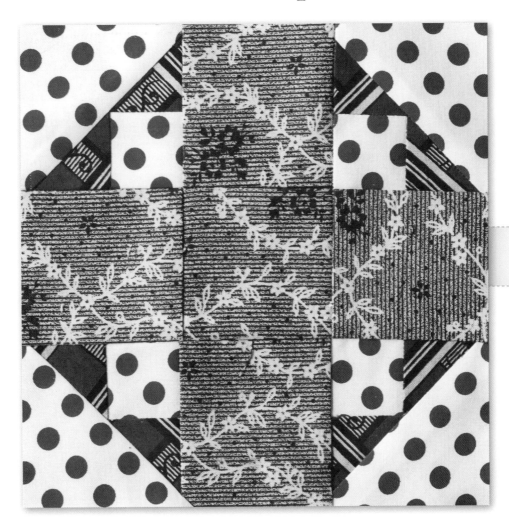

T-Square

Flying X Block

Broken Dishes

Path of Geese

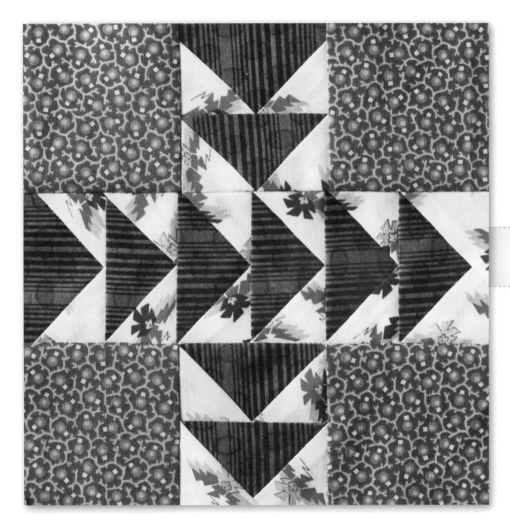

{ **A BIT OF HISTORY** Medallion quilts are designed around a center block that can be pieced, appliquéd or feature a toile. Borders are added until the quilter feels the quilt is finished. In addition to this block, great choices for the center block for a medallion would be Star in a Star (4), Doris's Delight Star (27), Beginner's Delight (65) and Rambler (176).

Economy Block

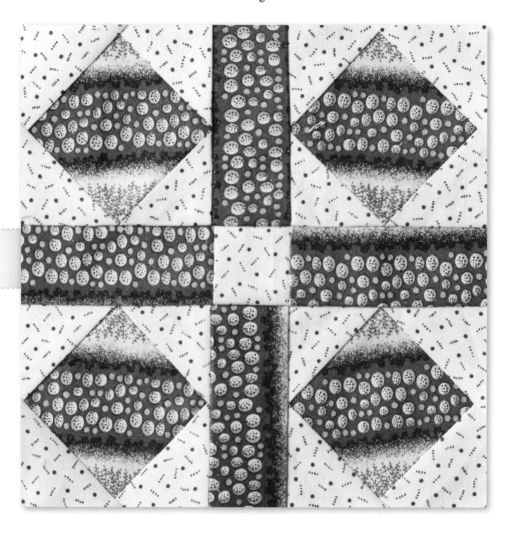

Squares and Rectangles

Large Double Nine Patch

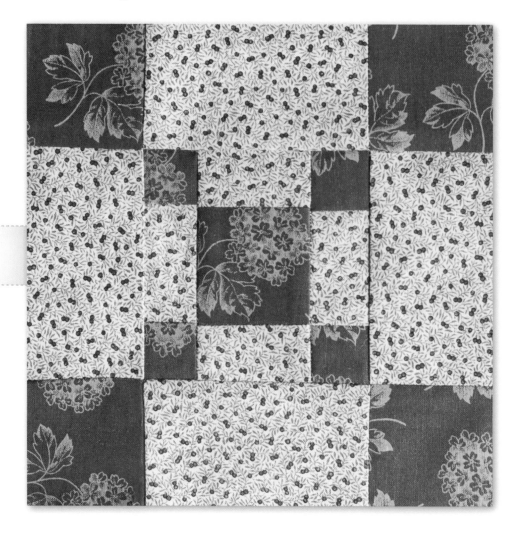

Thrifty Nine Patch

blocks with curves

B*locks with curves create visual movement in your quilt top. They are usually simple in design and can be hand or machine pieced together.*

Wheel

Indiana Puzzle

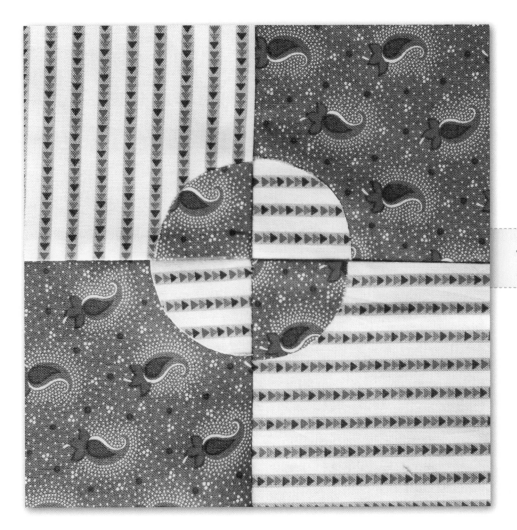

Fair Play

Baseball Diamond

Joseph's Coat

{ **DID YOU KNOW?** During the 1940s and 1950s, appliqué kits became popular. A quilter could purchase a kit in which the appliqué pieces were stamped and ready to be cut out and appliquéd to a prestamped top.

Curved Snowball

Pincushion

Spinning Nine Patch

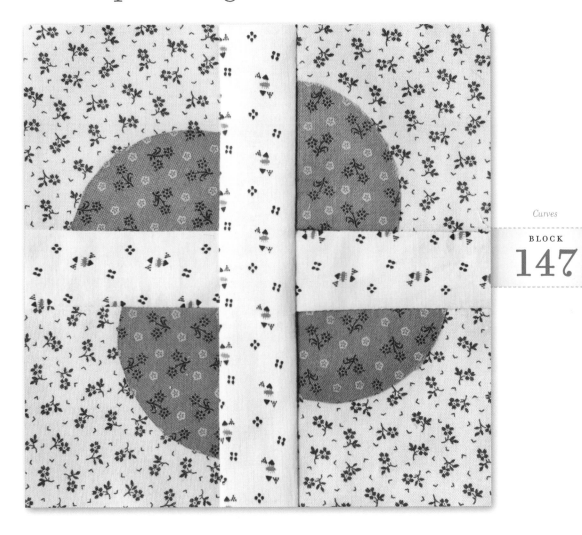

Dahlia

Rob Peter and Pay Paul

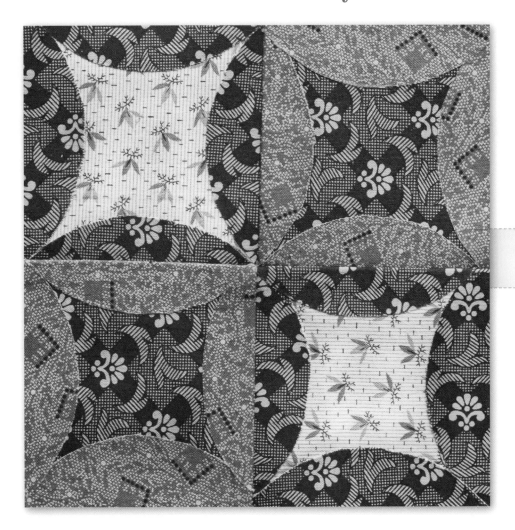

Fans

Curves

BLOCK
150

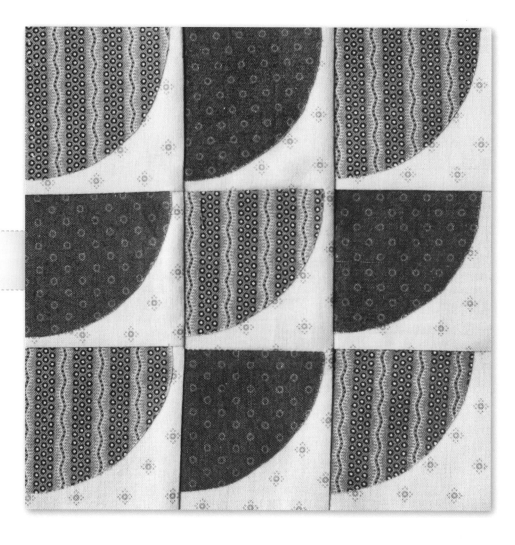

Dove

{ **DID YOU KNOW?** "Quiltings" or quilting parties became popular in the 1800s. Women got together to sew the blocks for the quilt top, and then sitting together around a frame, quilt the top.

blocks on point and square-in-a-square blocks

Blocks on point can add additional design interest to a quilt. Blocks on point and square-in-a-square blocks are not only visually appealing, they are easy to piece together. Beginners may have success using paper piecing methods to make square-in-a-square blocks.

Square on Point

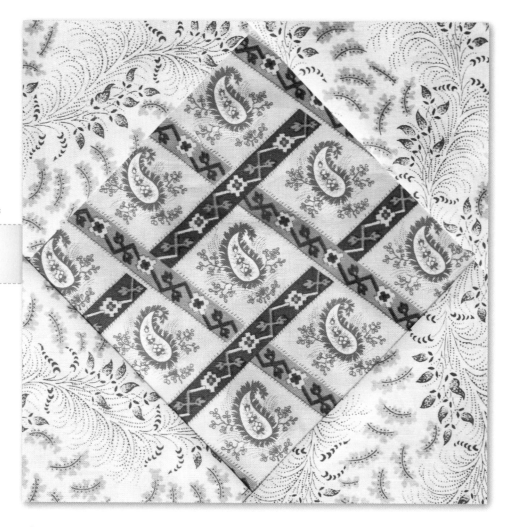

A BIT OF HISTORY Large squares or rectangles were typically used in utilitarian quilts. These practical quilts were usually tied with string or yarn or simply quilted, and were often made with a thick batting for additional warmth.

Square-in-Square with Stripes

Blockade

Chinese Lanterns

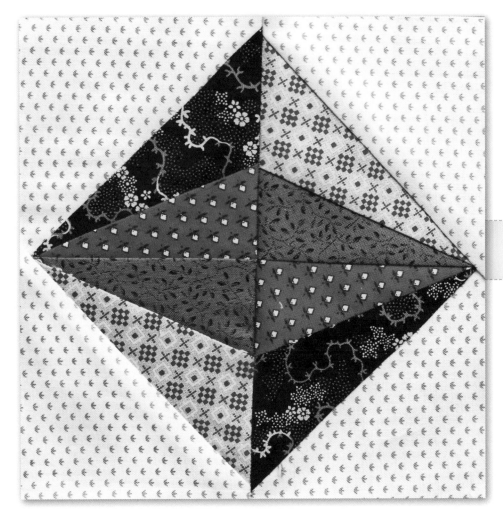

Art Square

Square-in-Squares

BLOCK
156

New Jersey

Double Anchor

Square-in-Squares

BLOCK
158

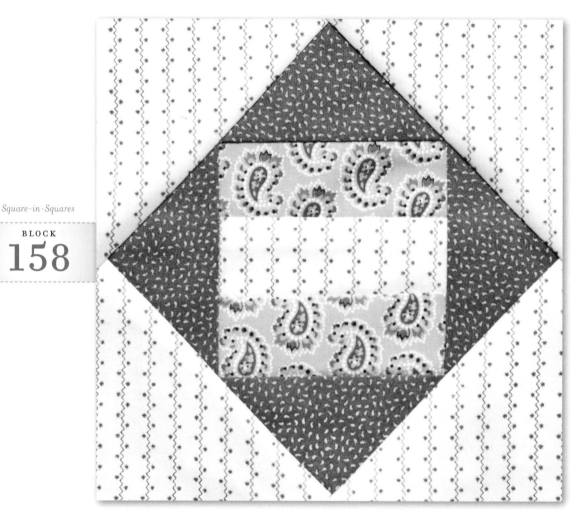

A BIT OF HISTORY Friendship quilts sprung up around 1840. Sometimes they were made with different blocks, and sometimes they were made using the same block. A friendship block is usually signed or dated. Favorite sayings or poems are sometimes added. In addition to this block, great blocks for a friendship quilt are Album Star (15), Signature Star (17) and Friendship Star (19).

Rotated Hourglass

Bobbin

Buzzard's Roost

Right and Left

Left and Right

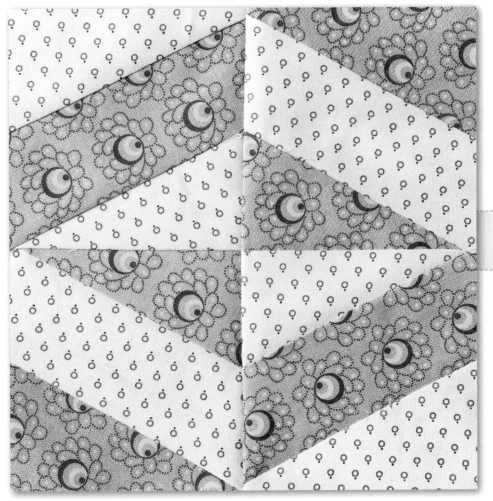

Scrap Block

Boy's Nonsense

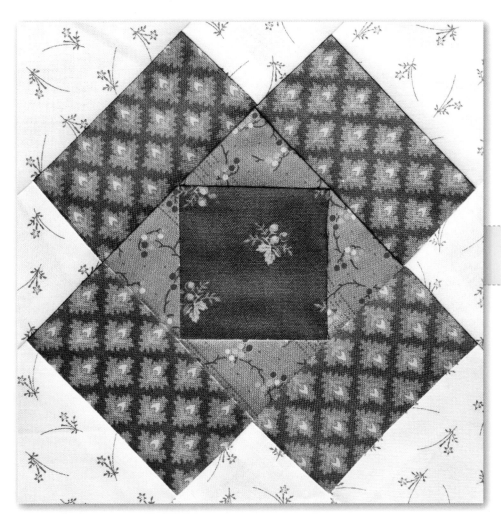

Checkerboard on Point

Snail's Trail

Double-Cross

{ DID YOU KNOW? In 1933, Sears, Roebuck & Company announced a quilt contest with a $1,000 prize for the first place winner. More than 25,000 quilts were entered. Today, quilters enter various quilt contests throughout the year with the top prize often $10,000–$20,000.

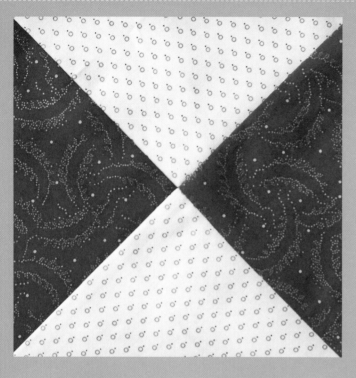

x blocks

An X block is composed of triangles, squares or rectangles that come together to form an X. Use these X blocks in your sampler or alone to create a beautiful quilt.

The X

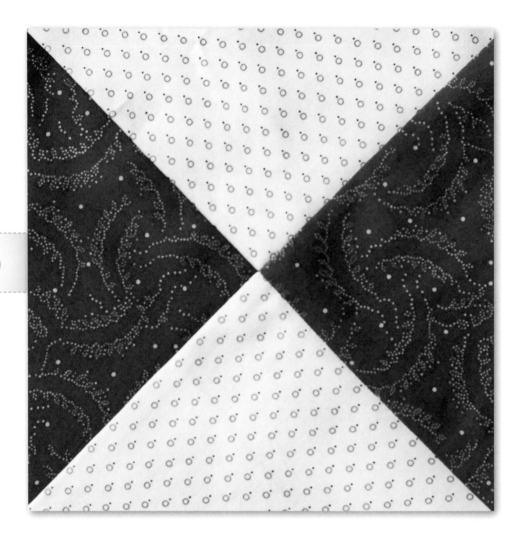

Lattice

Good Fortune

The House That Jack Built

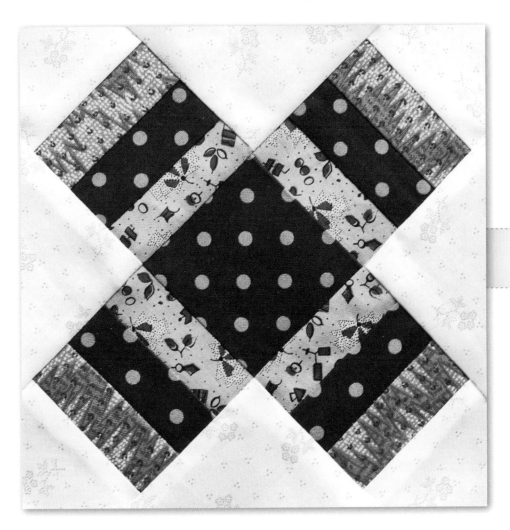

Light and Dark

DID YOU KNOW? Sewing circle societies often gathered at churches in the 1800s to make quilts for the poor in their city. That tradition continues today as women and men gather to make quilts for orphanages, veterans or communities that have suffered a catastrophe.

Star and Blocks

North Carolina Beauty

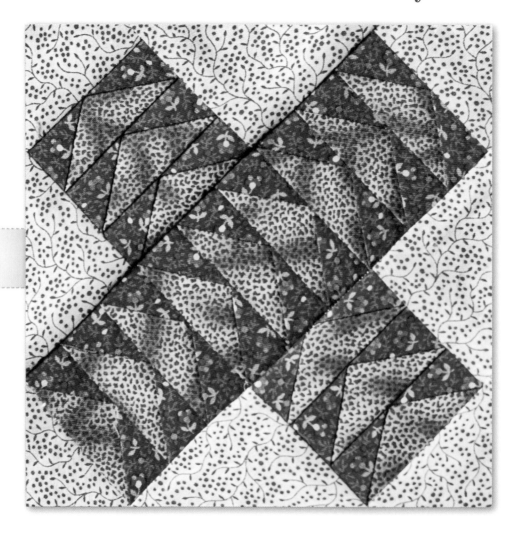

Rambler

At the Depot

Railroad Crossing

Paths

Arrowhead

X Outline

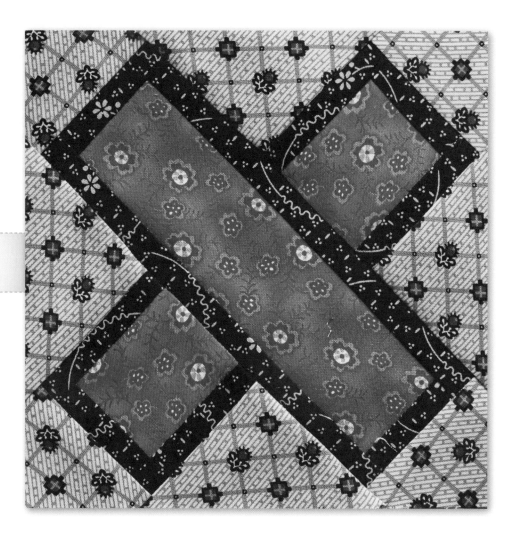

X Star Block

leftover favorites

T*raditional blocks such as the Log Cabin, T Block and Attic Window can be used alone or together to create the overall design of your quilt.*

Lantern

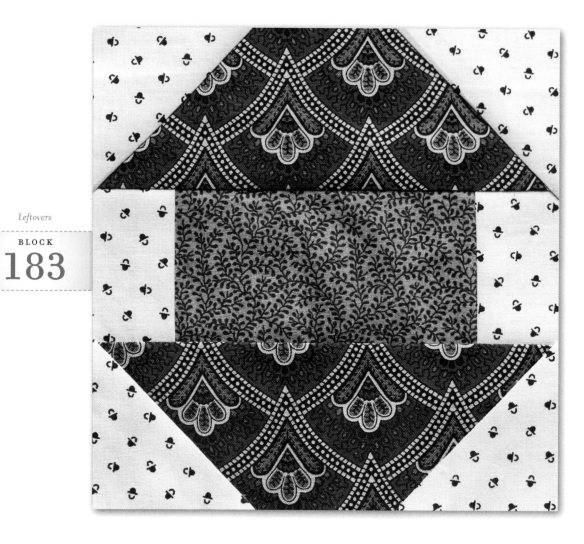

T Block

Log Cabin

{ **A BIT OF HISTORY** The Log Cabin block was popular in the late 1800s. Traditionally, the center square of each log cabin block was red in color. This center was surrounded by fabric strips or the logs. The Log Cabin block symbolized the pioneer spirit after the Civil War.

Basket

Leftovers

BLOCK

186

{ **A BIT OF HISTORY** Basket quilts appeared in different sizes and shapes throughout quilting history. Sometimes appliquéd flowers and fruit appeared in the quilt blocks. Basket quilts can also be made as a pieced block of triangles with an appliquéd handle.

Wild Goose Log Cabin

Diamond in Log Cabin

Courthouse Steps

Leftovers

BLOCK

189

Attic Window

Flying Geese

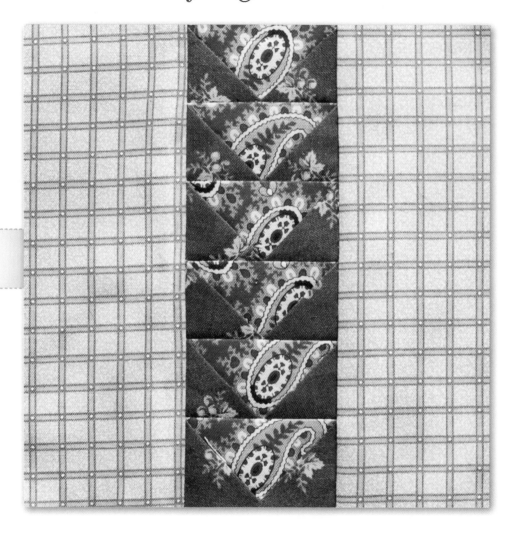

Snowball

Letter H

Lady of the Lake

Leftovers

BLOCK

194

Cracker

Scrappy String Star

Checkerboard

Leftovers

BLOCK
197

Flying Geese Strip

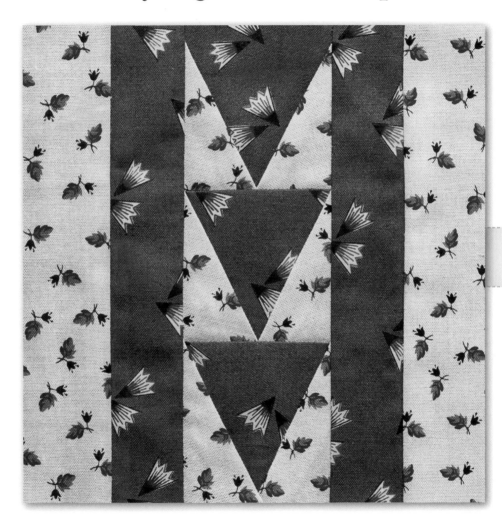

Four-Strip Rail Fence

Leftovers

BLOCK

199

Rectangles and Squares

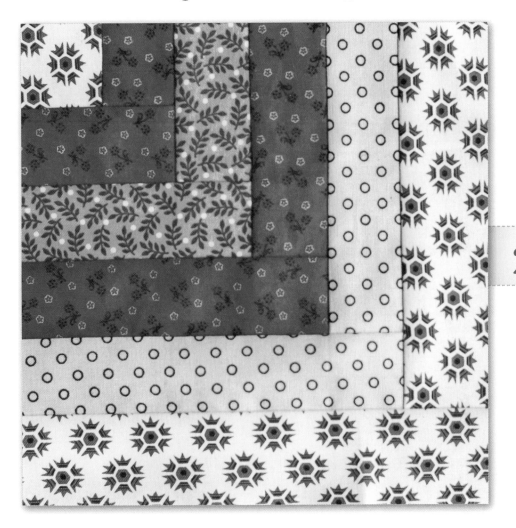

Lantern Light

Square Puzzle

quilts and projects

Simply Blocks

Made by the author. Machine quilted by Jennifer Delaney.
Finished size: 103½" × 110½" (263cm × 281cm)

FABRIC REQUIREMENTS

- Lattice fabric: 2¾ yards (2.5m)
- Cornerstone fabric: ½ yard (0.5m)
- Border fabric: 3¼ yards (3m)
- Binding fabric: 1¼ yards (1.1m)
- Backing fabric: 9¾ yards (8.9m)
- Block fabrics: Various fat quarters of coordinating fabrics for the blocks
- Batting

CUTTING INSTRUCTIONS

From the lattice fabric, cut:

- (337) 1½" × 6½" (4cm × 17cm) lattice strips

From the cornerstone fabric, cut:

- (182) 1½" × 1½" (4cm × 4cm) cornerstones

From the border fabric, cut lengthwise:

- (2) 9½" × 85½" (24cm × 217cm) outer border strips
- (2) 9½" × 110½" (24cm × 281cm) outer border strips

From the binding fabric, cut:

- (12) 2" × Width of Fabric (5cm × Width of Fabric) strips

From the backing fabric, cut:

- (3) 3¼ yards × Width of Fabric (3m × Width of Fabric)

ASSEMBLY INSTRUCTIONS

1 Make 156 blocks.

2 Sew the blocks into thirteen rows of twelve blocks each, with a lattice strip between each block and at the beginning and end of the row. Each row should have twelve blocks and thirteen lattice strips.

3 Sew together thirteen cornerstones alternating with twelve lattice strips to create a joining row. Sew fourteen joining rows in this way.

4 Matching the seams of the cornerstones with the seams of the lattice strips, sew the joining rows and block rows together in an alternating pattern, beginning and ending with a joining row. Your project should measure 85½" × 92½" (217cm × 235cm).

5 Sew a short border strip to the top and bottom of the quilt. Then sew a long border strip to the sides of the quilt.

6 Follow the Finishing the Project instructions located at the beginning of the book to baste, quilt and bind your quilt.

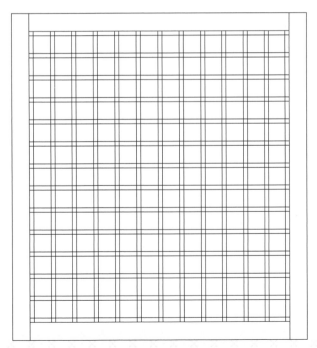

Assembly Diagram

Confetti General

FABRIC REQUIREMENTS

- Lattice fabric: 2 yards (1.8m)
- Cornerstone fabric: ½ yard (0.5m)
- Border fabric: 3 yards (2.7m)
- Binding fabric: 1¼ yard (1.1m)
- Backing fabric: 10½ yards (9.6m)
- Block fabrics: Various fat quarters of coordinating fabrics for the blocks
- Batting

Made by Carolyn Vidal. Machine quilted by Roxanne Eneroth.

Finished size: 90½" × 97½" (230cm × 248cm)

CUTTING INSTRUCTIONS

From the lattice fabric, cut:

- (287) 1½" × 6½" (4cm × 17cm) lattice strips

From the cornerstone fabric, cut:

- (156) 1½" × 1½" (4cm × 4cm) cornerstones

From the border fabric, cut lengthwise:

- (2) 6½" × 78½" (17cm × 199cm) border strips
- (2) 6½" × 97½" (17cm × 248cm) border strips

From the binding fabric, cut:

- (10) 2" × Width of Fabric (5cm × Width of Fabric) strips

From the backing fabric, cut:

- (3) 3½ yards × Width of Fabric (3.2m × Width of Fabric) sections

ASSEMBLY INSTRUCTIONS

1 Make 132 blocks.

2 Sew the blocks into twelve rows of eleven blocks each with a lattice strip between each block and at the beginning and end of the row. Each row should have eleven blocks and twelve lattice strips.

3 Sew together twelve cornerstones alternating with eleven lattice strips to create a joining row. Sew thirteen joining rows in this way.

4 Matching the seams of the cornerstones with the seams of the lattice strips, sew the joining rows and block rows together in an alternating pattern, beginning and ending with a joining row. Your project should measure 78.5" × 85.5" (199cm × 217cm).

5 Sew a long border strip to the sides of the quilt.

6 Follow the Finishing the Project instructions located at the beginning of the book to baste, quilt and bind your quilt.

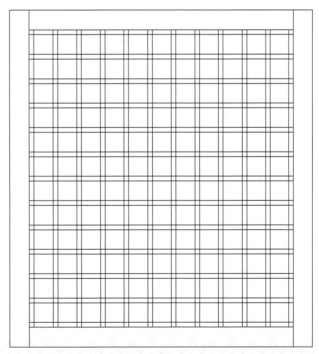

Assembly Diagram

Summer Batik Sampler

FABRIC REQUIREMENTS

- Lattice fabric: 1⅜ yards (1.3m)

- Cornerstone fabric: ½ yard (0.5m)

- Border fabric: 2⅛ yards (5.4m)

- Binding fabric: 1 yard (0.9m)

- Backing fabric: 5⅛ yards (4.7m)

- Block fabrics: Various fat quarters of coordinating fabrics for the blocks

- Batting

Made by Susan Price. Machine quilted by Valerie Langue.

Finished size: 62½" × 83½" (159cm × 212cm)

CUTTING INSTRUCTIONS

From the lattice fabric, cut:

- (157) 1½" × 6½" (4cm × 17cm) lattice strips

From the cornerstone fabric, cut:

- (88) 1½" × 1½" (4cm × 4cm) cornerstones

From the border fabric, cut lengthwise:

- (2) 6½" × 50½" (17cm × 128cm) border strips
- (2) 6½" × 83½" (17cm × 212cm) border strips

From the binding fabric, cut:

- (10) 2" × Width of Fabric (5cm × Width of Fabric) strips

From the backing fabric, cut:

- (2) 2⅜ yards × Width of Fabric (2.4m × Width of Fabric) sections

ASSEMBLY INSTRUCTIONS

1 Make 70 blocks.

2 Sew the blocks into ten rows of seven blocks each, with a lattice strip between each block and at the beginning and end of the row. Each row should have seven blocks and eight lattice strips.

3 Sew together eight cornerstones alternating with seven lattice strips to create a joining row. Sew eleven joining rows in this way.

4 Matching the seams of the cornerstones with the seams of the lattice strips, sew the joining rows and block rows together in an alternating pattern, beginning and ending with a joining row. Your project should measure 50½" × 71½" (128cm × 182cm).

5 Sew a short border strip to the top and bottom of the quilt. Then sew a long border strip to both sides of the quilt.

6 Follow the Finishing the Project instructions located at the beginning of the book to baste, quilt and bind your quilt.

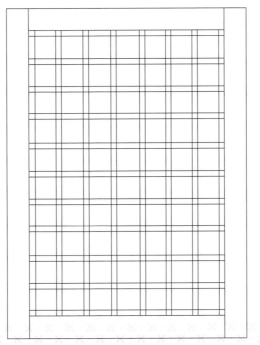

Assembly Diagram

The Victoria

Made by Amy Stevens.

Finished size: 54½" × 60½" (138cm × 154cm)

FABRIC REQUIREMENTS

- Border and column strip fabric: 3 yards (2.7m)
- Binding fabric: 1 yard (0.9m)
- Backing fabric: 3½ yards (3.2m)
- Block fabrics: Various fat quarters of coordinating fabrics for the blocks
- Batting

CUTTING INSTRUCTIONS

From the border and column strip fabric, cut lengthwise:

- (5) 6½" × 48½" (17cm × 123cm) column strips
- (2) 6½" × 54½" (17cm × 138cm) border strips

From the binding fabric, cut:

- (8) 2" × Width of Fabric (5cm × Width of Fabric) strips

From the backing fabric, cut:

- (2) 1¾ yards × Width of Fabric (1.6m × Width of Fabric) sections

ASSEMBLY INSTRUCTIONS

1 Make 32 blocks and assemble the blocks into four columns of eight blocks each. Each row should measure 48½" (123cm) long.

2 Alternating back and forth, sew together the five column strips and four block strips. Your quilt should now measure 48½" × 54½" (123cm × 138cm).

3 Sew a remaining long border strip to the top and bottom of the quilt.

4 Follow the Finishing the Project instructions at the beginning of the book to baste, quilt and bind your quilt.

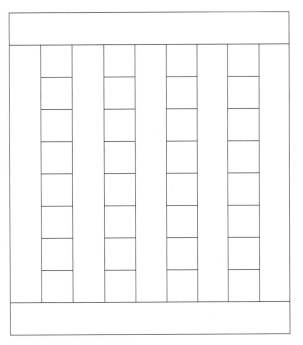

Assembly Diagram

Fig Tree Sampler

FABRIC REQUIREMENTS

- Lattice and inner border fabric: ¾ yard (0.7m)

- Cornerstone fabric: ¼ yard (0.2m)

- Outer border fabric: 2 yards (1.8m)

- Binding fabric: 1 yard (0.9m)

- Backing fabric: 3½ yards (3.2m)

- Block fabrics: Various fat quarters of coordinating fabrics for the blocks

- Batting

Made by Connie Makl. Machine quilted by Judy Becker.

Finished size: 48½" × 62½" (123cm × 159cm)

CUTTING INSTRUCTIONS

From the lattice fabric, cut:

- (58) 1½" × 6½" (4cm × 17cm) lattice strips

From the cornerstone fabric, cut:

- (24) 1½" × 1½" (4cm × 4cm) cornerstones

From the inner border fabric, cut and piece:

- (2) 1½" × 34½" (4cm × 88cm) inner border strips
- (2) 1½" × 50½" (4cm × 128cm) inner border strips

From the outer border fabric, cut lengthwise:

- (2) 6½" × 36½" (17cm × 93cm) outer border strips
- (2) 6½" × 62½" (17cm × 159cm) outer border strips

From the binding fabric, cut:

- (7) 2" × Width of Fabric (5cm × Width of Fabric) strips

From the backing fabric, cut:

- (2) 1¾ yards × Width of Fabric (1.6m × Width of Fabric) sections

ASSEMBLY INSTRUCTIONS

1 Make 35 blocks.

2 Sew the blocks into seven rows of five blocks each, with a lattice strip between each block. Each row should have five blocks and four lattice strips.

3 Sew together five lattice strips alternating with four cornerstones to create a joining row. Sew six joining rows in this way.

4 Matching the seams of the cornerstones with the seams of the lattice strips, sew the joining rows and block rows together in an alternating pattern. Your project should measure 34½" × 48½" (88cm × 123cm).

5 Sew a long inner border strip to the top and bottom of the quilt. Then sew a short inner border strip to both sides of the quilt. Sew the outer border strips to the quilt in the same way.

6 Follow the Finishing the Project instructions at the beginning of the book to baste, quilt and bind your quilt.

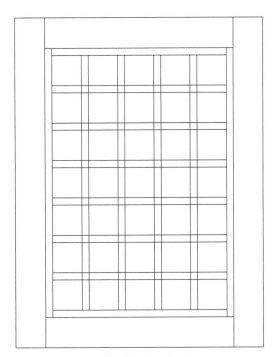

Assembly Diagram

American Dream

Made by Jeanne Meddaugh. Machine quilted by Judy Becker.
Finished size: 37½" × 37½" (95cm × 95cm)

FABRIC REQUIREMENTS

- Lattice fabric: ½ yard (0.5m)
- Cornerstone fabric: ⅛ yard (0.1m)
- Border fabric: 1¼ yards (1.1m)
- Binding fabric: 1 yard (0.9m)
- Backing fabric: 1¼ yards (1.1m)
- Block fabrics: Various fat quarters of coordinating fabrics for the blocks
- Batting

CUTTING INSTRUCTIONS

From the lattice fabric, cut:

- (40) 1½" × 6½" (4cm × 17cm) lattice strips

From the cornerstone fabric, cut:

- (25) 1½" × 1½" (4cm × 4cm) cornerstones

From the border fabric, cut:

- (2) 4½" × 29½" (11cm × 75cm) border strips
- (2) 4½" × 37½" (11cm × 95cm) border strips

From the binding fabric, cut:

- (4) 2" × Width of Fabric (5cm × Width of Fabric) strips

From the backing fabric, cut:

- 42" × 42" (107cm × 107cm) section

ASSEMBLY INSTRUCTIONS

1 Make 16 blocks.

2 Sew the blocks into four rows of four blocks each, with a lattice strip between each block and at the beginning and end of the row. Each row should have four blocks and five lattice strips.

3 Sew together five cornerstones alternating with four lattice strips to create a joining row. Sew five joining rows in this way.

4 Matching the seams of the cornerstones with the seams of the lattice strips, sew the joining rows and block rows together in an alternating pattern, beginning and ending with a joining row. Your project should measure 29½" × 29½" (75cm × 75cm).

5 Sew a short border strip to both sides of the quilt. Then sew a long border strip to the top and bottom of the quilt.

6 Follow the Finishing the Project instructions at the beginning of the book to quilt and bind your quilt.

Note: If you'd like, add a scallop border to this quilt as the designer did. Simply figure out how many scallops you would like on each side of the border, and then draw scallops on all four sides of the quilt, making sure they are evenly spaced. After your quilt is quilted, cut out your scallops and bind.

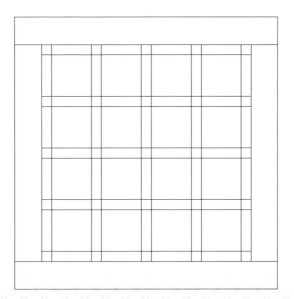

Assembly Diagram

Block Euphoria

FABRIC REQUIREMENTS

- Lattice and inner border fabric: ½ yard (0.5m)

- Cornerstone fabric: ⅛ yard (0.1m)

- Outer border fabric: ¾ yard (0.7m)

- Binding fabric: ¼ yard (0.2m)

- Backing fabric: 1½ yards (1.4m)

- Block fabrics: Various fat quarters of coordinating fabrics for the blocks and border corners

- Batting

Made and quilted by Karen Weilder.
Finished size: 30½" × 44½" (78cm × 103cm)

CUTTING INSTRUCTIONS

From the lattice and inner border fabric, cut:

- (22) 1½" × 6½" (4cm × 17cm) lattice strips
- (2) 1½" × 20½" (4cm × 52cm) inner border strips
- (2) 1½" × 36½" (4cm × 93cm) inner border strips

From the cornerstone fabric, cut:

- (8) 1½" × 1½" (4cm × 4cm) cornerstones

From the outer border fabric, cut:

- (2) 4½" × 22½" (11cm × 57cm) outer border strips
- (2) 4½" × 36½" (11cm × 93cm) outer border strips

From the binding fabric, cut:

- (4) 2" × Width of Fabric (5cm × Width of Fabric) strips

From the backing fabric, cut:

- 38" × 52" (97cm × 132cm) backing section

From the various fat quarters, cut:

- (4) 4½" × 4½" (11cm × 11cm) corner squares, or piece four blocks that measure 4½" × 4½" (11cm × 11cm) unfinished

ASSEMBLY INSTRUCTIONS

1 Make 15 blocks.

2 Sew the blocks into five rows of three blocks each, with a lattice strip between each block. Each row should have three blocks and two lattice strips.

3 Sew together three lattice strips alternating with two cornerstones to create a joining row. Sew four joining rows in this way.

4 Matching the seams of the cornerstones with the seams of the lattice strips, sew the joining rows and block rows together in an alternating pattern. Your project should measure 20½" × 34½" (52cm × 88cm).

5 Sew a short inner border strip to the top and bottom of the quilt. Then sew a long inner border strip to both sides of the quilt.

6 Sew a 4½" (11cm) block to each end of both outer border strips and press. Sew the outer border strips to the quilt in the same way as the inner border strips.

7 Follow the Finishing the Project instructions at the beginning of the book to quilt and bind your quilt.

Note: The outer border fabric in this quilt is striped to achieve an easy piano-key look.

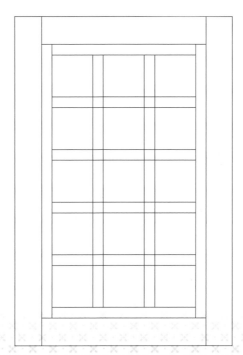

Assembly Diagram

Quilt Blanket

Made by Sarah Youngs.

Finished size: 30½" × 37½" (78cm × 95cm)

FABRIC REQUIREMENTS

- Lattice fabric: ⅜ yard (0.3m)
- Cornerstone fabric: ⅛ yard (0.1m)
- Border fabric: 1⅛ yard (1m)
- Backing fabric: 1½ yards (1.4m)
- Block fabrics: Various fat quarters of coordinating fabrics for the blocks
- Binding: *There is no binding for this quilt as the quilt and the backing are placed right sides together, stitched and then turned inside out through an opening.*

CUTTING INSTRUCTIONS

From the lattice fabric, cut:

- (31) 1½" × 6½" (4cm × 17cm) lattice strips

From the cornerstone fabric, cut:

- (20) 1½" × 1½" (4cm × 4cm) cornerstones

From the border fabric, cut:

- (2) 4½" × 22½" (11cm × 57cm) border strips
- (2) 4½" × 37½" (11cm × 95cm) border strips

From the backing fabric, cut:

- 33" × 40" (84cm × 102cm) backing piece

ASSEMBLY INSTRUCTIONS

1 Make 12 blocks.

2 Sew the blocks into four rows of three blocks each, with a lattice strip between each block and at the beginning and end of the row. Each row should have three blocks and four lattice strips.

3 Sew together four cornerstones alternating with three lattice strips to create a joining row. Sew five joining rows in this way.

4 Matching the seams of the cornerstones with the seams of the lattice strips, sew the joining rows and block rows together in an alternating pattern, beginning and ending with a joining row. Your project should measure 22½" × 29½" (57cm × 75cm).

5 Sew a border strip to the top and bottom of the quilt. Then sew a border strip to both sides of the quilt.

6 Follow the Finishing the Project instructions at the beginning of the book to finish this quilt as a Quilt Blanket.

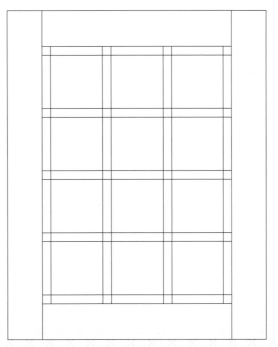

Assembly Diagram

Tulip Garden

Made by Solomyn Collen. Quilted by Solomyn Collen and Rita Collen.

Finished Size: 30½" × 30½" ((78cm × 78cm)

FABRIC REQUIREMENTS

- Lattice fabric: ¼ yard (0.2m)
- Cornerstone fabric: ⅛ yard (0.1m)
- Border fabric: ¾ yard (0.7m)
- Binding fabric: ⅜ yard (0.3m)
- Backing fabric: 1 yard (0.9m)
- Block fabrics: Various fat quarters of coordinating fabrics for the blocks
- Batting

CUTTING INSTRUCTIONS

From the lattice fabric, cut:

- (24) 1½" × 6½" (4cm × 17cm) lattice strips

From the cornerstone fabric, cut:

- (16) 1½" × 1½" (4cm × 4cm) cornerstones

From the border fabric, cut:

- (2) 4½" × 22½" (11cm × 57cm) border strips
- (2) 4½" × 30½" (11cm × 78cm) border strips

From the binding fabric, cut:

- (4) 2" × Width of Fabric (5cm × Width of Fabric) strips

From the backing fabric, cut:

- 36" × 36" (91cm × 91cm) backing piece

ASSEMBLY INSTRUCTIONS

1 Make 9 blocks.

2 Sew the blocks into three rows of three blocks each, with a lattice strip between each block and at the beginning and end of the row. Each row should have three blocks and four lattice strips.

3 Sew together four cornerstones alternating with three lattice strips to create a joining row. Sew four joining rows in this way.

4 Matching the seams of the cornerstones with the seams of the lattice strips, sew the joining rows and block rows together in an alternating pattern, beginning and ending with a joining row. Your project should measure 22½" × 22½" (57cm × 57cm).

5 Sew a border strip to both sides of the quilt. Then sew a border strip to the top and bottom of the quilt.

6 Follow the Finishing the Project instructions at the beginning of the book to baste, quilt and bind your quilt.

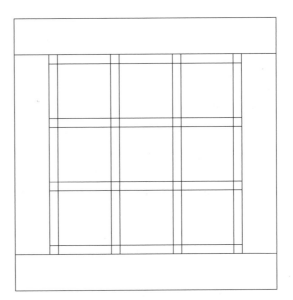

Assembly Diagram

Hailey's Table Topper

FABRIC REQUIREMENTS

- Lattice fabric: ¼ yard (0.2m)
- Cornerstone fabric: ⅛ yard (0.1m)
- Border fabric: ¾ yard (0.7m)
- Binding fabric: ¼ yard (0.2m)
- Backing fabric: ¾ yard (0.7m)
- Block fabrics: Various fat quarters of coordinating fabrics for the blocks
- Batting

Made by Hailey Clack.

Finished size: 23½" × 37½" (60cm × 95cm)

CUTTING INSTRUCTIONS

From the lattice fabric, cut:

- (22) 1½" × 6½" (4cm × 17cm) lattice strips

From the cornerstone fabric, cut:

- (15) 1½" × 1½" (4cm × 4cm) cornerstones

From the border fabric, cut:

- (2) 4½" × 15½" (11cm × 39cm) border strips
- (2) 4½" × 37½" (11cm × 95cm) border strips

From the binding fabric, cut:

- (4) 2" × Width of Fabric (5cm × Width of Fabric) strips

From the backing fabric, cut:

- 1 yard × Width of Fabric (0.9m × Width of Fabric) backing piece

ASSEMBLY INSTRUCTIONS

1 Make 8 blocks.

2 Sew the blocks into four rows of two blocks each, with a lattice strip between each block and at the beginning and end of the row. Each row should have two blocks and three lattice strips.

3 Sew together three cornerstones alternating with two lattice strips to create a joining row. Sew five joining rows in this way.

4 Matching the seams of the cornerstones with the seams of the lattice strips, sew the joining rows and block rows together in an alternating pattern, beginning and ending with a joining row. Your project should measure 15½" × 29½" (39cm × 75cm).

5 Sew a border strip to the top and bottom of the quilt. Then sew a border strip to the sides of the quilt.

6 Follow the Finishing the Project instructions at the beginning of the book to baste, quilt and bind your quilt.

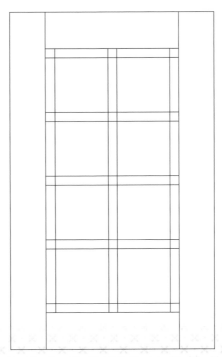

Assembly Diagram

Sophia's Table Topper

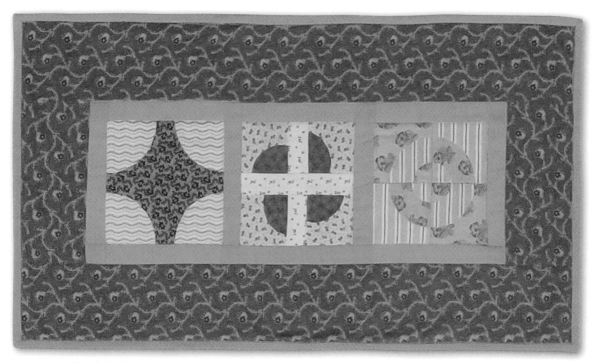

Made by Sophia Clack.

Finished size: 16½" × 30½" (42cm × 78cm)

FABRIC REQUIREMENTS

- Lattice fabric: ¼ yard (0.2m)

- Cornerstone fabric: ⅛ yard (0.1m)

- Border fabric: ⅓ yard (0.3m)

- Binding fabric: ¼ yard (0.2m)

- Backing fabric: ¾ yard (0.7m)

- Block fabrics: Various fat quarters of coordinating fabrics for the blocks

- Batting

CUTTING INSTRUCTIONS

From the lattice fabric, cut:

- (10) 1½" × 6½" (4cm × 17cm) lattice strips

From the cornerstone fabric, cut:

- (8) 1½" × 1½" (4cm × 4cm) cornerstones

From the border fabric, cut:

- (2) 4½" × 8½" (11cm × 22cm) border strips
- (2) 4½" × 30½" (11cm × 78cm) border strips

From the binding fabric, cut:

- (3) 2" × Width of Fabric (5cm × Width of Fabric) strips

From the backing fabric, cut:

- 36" × 22" (91cm × 56cm) backing piece

ASSEMBLY INSTRUCTIONS

1 Make 3 blocks.

2 Sew three blocks together with a lattice strip in between each block and at the beginning and end of the row. The row should have three blocks and four lattice strips.

3 Sew together four cornerstones alternating with three lattice strips to create a joining row. Sew two joining rows in this way.

4 Matching the seams of the cornerstones with the seams of the lattice strips, sew a joining row to the top and the bottom of the block row. Your project should measure 8½" × 22½" (22cm × 57cm).

5 Sew a border strip to both sides of the quilt. Then sew a border strip to the top and bottom of the quilt.

6 Follow the Finishing the Project instructions at the beginning of the book to baste, quilt and bind your quilt.

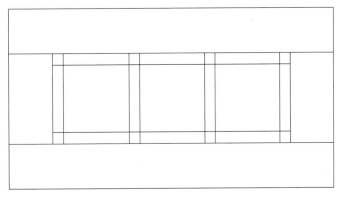

Assembly Diagram

Contributors

HAILEY CLACK
Hailey is 9 years old and learned to quilt from her Nana, Rosemary. She enjoys quilting and has helped her Nana on many different projects, helping to make dresses and quilts for orphans and clothes for her dolls. Hailey enjoys riding her bike, playing with her friends and spending time with her cousins.

SOPHIA CLACK
Sophia is 7 years old and just started quilting this year. This quilt is Sophia's first finished project. Over the last year, she has helped piece squares for quilts given to an orphanage in Ethiopia. Sophia enjoys reading, playing with her friends, frog and turtle catching at the campground and riding her bike.

SOLOMYN COLLEN
Solomyn Collen is 11 years old. In her spare time she likes to read, quilt, sew, play with her two pet mice, knit, scrapbook and listen to music. She loves stuffed animals, puppets, Coca-Cola, chocolate fudge, mice, rats and dogs.

CONNIE MAKL
I began quilting in the late 1970s, and it didn't take long for me to fall in love with all aspects of the craft. I love traditional quilts, both pieced and appliqué, as well as miniatures and quilts using Civil War fabrics. I have met many wonderful people along my journey and am thankful for the friendships I have made.

JEANNE MEDDAUGH
Through quilting, I have made friends all over the world. Scrappy quilts are my favorite to make and the nine patch block is always a winner in my book. Reproduction fabrics appeal to me the most, as well as little quilts. It is a privilege to make a quilt using blocks from Rosemary's book.

SUSAN LAITY PRICE

I enjoy all type of needlework, but once rotary cutting techniques were developed, quilting took over my creative life. Trying new techniques and colors keeps quilting fresh and exciting. I have enjoyed making sampler quilts from two of Rosemary's previous books using 1800s reproduction fabrics. Being able to choose my favorite blocks and make the quilt fit my size requirements is one of the greatest things about sampler quilts.

AMY STEVENS

As a child, I remember my mom leaning over the quilting frame as she worked on quilts for me. Today, I enjoy sewing, particularly embroidery. To me, embroidery is less complicated than matching up seams and making everything the right size.

CAROLYN VIDAL

I have been sewing and quilting for sixty years. My first quilting memories are of rocking the treadle under my grandmother's feet as she sewed. She would patiently say, "Go, Kitty. Stop, Kitty." I still look at the dolly quilt she helped me make from old clothes and get sentimental remembering who wore what. That began my lifetime love of sewing and quilting. This quilt was a labor of two loves: Rosemary's blocks and French General (for Moda) fabrics.

KAREN WEILDER

I have been quilting for about twenty-five years. I prefer to work with traditional blocks, reproduction fabrics and shirtings. I have too much fabric, too many projects, too many books and not enough time! Quilting is my thing—I love it.

SARAH YOUNGS

Sarah is from West Michigan. She is a wife and a mother to two children. She began sewing a few years ago, and quilting soon became one of her favorite hobbies.

ABOUT THE AUTHOR

Rosemary Youngs has been quilting since the 1980s. Her quilts have won numerous awards in local and major quilt shows. Pictures of her work have been published in various books and magazines. She has taught at local shops and enjoys designing quilts that tell stories. Her first book, *The Amish Circle Quilt*, tells the story of eleven Amish women, their culture and their quilting. *The Civil War Diary Quilt*, *The Civil War Love Letter Quilt* and *The Civil War Anniversary Quilt* contain diaries and letters that were written during the Civil War. *Quilts from the American Homefront*, her fifth book in the series, was inspired by letters from World War II. Rosemary resides in Walker, Michigan, with her family.

18 17 16 15 14   5 4 3 2 1

DISTRIBUTED IN CANADA BY FRASER DIRECT
100 Armstrong Avenue
Georgetown, ON, Canada L7G 5S4
Tel: (905) 877-4411

DISTRIBUTED IN THE U.K. AND EUROPE
BY F+W MEDIA INTERNATIONAL
Brunel House, Newton Abbot, Devon, TQ12 4PU, England
Tel: (+44) 1626 323200, Fax: (+44) 1626 323319
Email: postmaster@davidandcharles.co.uk

DISTRIBUTED IN AUSTRALIA BY CAPRICORN LINK
P.O. Box 704, S. Windsor NSW, 2756 Australia
Tel: (02) 4577-3555

Edited by Kelly Biscopink

Designed by Julie Barnett

Production coordinated by Greg Nock

Photography by Stacey Clack
(Stacey Clack Photography)

www.fwmedia.com

METRIC CONVERSION CHART

TO CONVERT	TO	MULTIPLY BY
inches	centimeters	2.54
centimeters	inches	0.4
feet	centimeters	30.5
centimeters	feet	0.03
yards	meters	0.9
meters	yards	1.1

Index

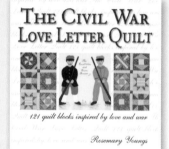